Happiness
for All?

Happiness for All?

Unequal Hopes and Lives in Pursuit of the American Dream

Carol Graham

WITHDRAWN
UTSA LIBRARIES

Princeton University Press

Princeton and Oxford

Copyright © 2017 by Princeton University Press
Published by Princeton University Press, 41 William Street,
Princeton, New Jersey 08540
In the United Kingdom: Princeton University Press,
6 Oxford Street, Woodstock, Oxfordshire OX20 1TR

press.princeton.edu

Jacket image courtesy of Shutterstock

ISBN 978-0-691-16946-0

Library of Congress Control Number: 2016961394

British Library Cataloging-in-Publication Data is available

This book has been composed in Garamond Premier Pro

Printed on acid-free paper. ∞

Printed in the United States of America

1 3 5 7 9 10 8 6 4 2

Dedication

To Anna, Adrian, and Alexander—
the true source of my hopes and dreams

Contents

Illustrations

Tables

Preface

I present this book with some trepidation. I have spent most of my career studying poverty, inequality, and, more recently, well-being around the world, with a focus on developing economies. Although I grew up partly in the United States (and am a U.S. citizen), I was born in Peru and have a strong grounding in each culture. This is my first large body of work that focuses primarily on the United States. There are many scholars who know much more about U.S. poverty and inequality than I do. Yet what I have been seeing, experiencing, reading, and finding in my data in recent years is too compelling for me to not write about it.

My book is a story of a country divided not only in terms of the distribution of income and opportunity, but also in terms of hopes and dreams. The United States is now much more divided on many fronts than the region where I was born.

Over forty years ago, my father wrote a seminal article in the Archives of Environmental Health titled "The High Costs of Being Poor." He and his coauthor documented the higher costs that the poor paid for essential services—such as purchasing water from trucks and using kerosene and candles in lieu of electricity. The poor paid roughly fifteen times more per unit on average than the wealthy paid for piped water and electricity, while the services they purchased, such as contaminated water, were clearly inferior. Not surprisingly the health outcomes of their children suffered. Now, those same urban slums where he—and later I—conducted research have access to public services and house a burgeoning middle class.

In this book, I focus on the high costs of being poor in the United States, costs that are usually not in the form of material goods or basic services, but in the form of stress, insecurity, and lack of hope. In part this is due to inadequate access to health insurance and stable jobs, and in part it is due to the increasing distance—in terms of income, education, and opportunities—between those at the top and bottom of the distribution. As in the case of inferior health outcomes for the children of the poor in Peru in the 1970s, the children of the poor in the United States today inherit insecurity and lack of hope.

There are endless articles and even some books on how unequal the country has become and how fragile the American Dream is. My story is different because of the metrics that I use to tell it. Rather than focusing on Gini coefficients, 90/10 ratios, and/or probabilities of moving up or down the income ladder (and I confess to using all of these terms throughout the book), my central focus is the unequal distribution of hopes, dreams, and expectations for the future, and why this is likely to lead to even more unequally shared outcomes in the future.

Individuals who believe in and have hope for the future invest in it; those who have no such hopes typically do not. Not only are their futures compromised as a result, but so are their children's. The markers of unequally shared hope in the United States are evident not only in the income, education, and employment data, but also in differences across socioeconomic cohorts in mortality and morbidity, marriage, and incarceration rates and other signs of societal fragmentation. They are even evident in the words that different cohorts use. The vocabulary of the wealthy reflects knowledge acquisition and health-conscious behaviors; that of the poor reflects desperation, short-term outlooks, and patchwork solutions.

This is a deep-seated and difficult problem to solve, and the answers are not obvious. I have no magic bullets to offer. My conclusions highlight the importance of identifying and measuring the extent of the problem. Well-being metrics can play an important role in monitoring trends in quality of life and life experiences, as well as in hope and aspirations on the one hand, and desperation and misery on the other. I also point to policies—including many experimental ones—that have improved economic outcomes and lives in general, with the provision of hope being an important channel. Well-being metrics can help in the design and evaluation of such policies. All of this, by definition, is work in progress, and my own research is exploring new kinds of interventions as this book goes to press.

There are a number of people that I must thank for either inspiring my work or commenting on it or both over the years. These include George Akerlof, Jeremy Barofsky, Nancy Birdsall, Gary Burtless, Laurence Chandy, Andrew Clark, Angus Deaton, Steven Durlauf, Richard Easterlin, Clifford Gaddy, Ross Hammond, Andrew Oswald, Jonathan Rauch, Richard Reeves, Jonathan Rothwell, Isabel Sawhill, and Peyton Young. In addition, I was lucky enough to serve on a National Academy of Sciences panel on well-being, and gained a completely new education about the psychological dimensions of well-being measurement from the wonderful scholars on the panel: Laura Carstensen, Danny Kahneman, and Arthur Stone.

I also have to thank Sarah Caro of Princeton University Press for being the best editor ever; she was absolutely critical to my *Happiness Around the World* book in 2009, and then helped inspire this one. I am also grateful to Hannah Paul at the press for her invaluable help, and to two anonymous reviewers for the very constructive comments. I also thank Jenny Wolkowicki and Joseph Dahm for careful and invaluable editorial assistance. At Brookings, a number of people have been essential to supporting my research on unusual topics and giving me confidence in doing so, as well as providing financial and administrative backing. These include Strobe Talbott, Charlotte Baldwin, Steve Bennett, Kim Churches, Kemal Dervis, Yamillet Fuentes, Martin Indyk, Homi Kharas, Aki Nemoto, Kristina Server, and Jen Banks. Finally, I could not have survived the past few years or written this book without the excellent research assistance and collaboration of Soumya Chattopadhyay, Milena Nikolova, Sergio Pinto, and Julia Ruiz-Pozuelo.

CHAPTER 1

Introduction

Happiness for All: Living the Dream?

Life should be better and richer and fuller for everyone, with opportunity for each according to ability and achievement regardless of social class or circumstances at birth.

—*James Thurlow Adams,* The Epic of America

Sukhov went off to sleep, and he was completely content. Fate had been kind in many ways that day; he hadn't been put in the cells, the gang had not been sent to the Socialist Community Center, he'd fiddled himself an extra bowl of porridge for dinner. . . . The day had gone by without a single cloud—almost a happy day. There were three thousand six hundred and fifty-three days like that in his sentence, from reveille to lights out. The three extra days were because of the leap years.

—*David Malouf, quoting Aleksandr Solzhenitsyn in* One Day in the Life of Ivan Denisovich

The U.S. Pledge of Allegiance promises liberty and justice for all. The U.S. Declaration of Independence guarantees the rights to life, liberty, and the pursuit of happiness to all citizens. These promises are not about guaranteed outcomes, but about opportunities to seek fulfilling lives. They have a long grounding in history and philosophy, beginning with Aristotle's concept of happiness. This concept—eudemonia—is not about contentment, but about having sufficient means to be able to seek purpose or meaning in life. When Jefferson conceived of the pursuit of happiness, he was grounded in the works of Plato and Aristotle, as well as in the kind of liberalism articulated by John Stuart Mill, which combines notions of individual freedom and societal fairness (Malouf, 2011; Reeves, 2007). These promises are the basis of the American Dream, with its strong focus on individual freedom, opportunity, and faith in future mobility.

Yet there is increasing debate—both academic and political—about the extent to which the American Dream—and the right to the pursuit of happiness—is equally available to all citizens today. U.S. trends in opportunity and in distributional outcomes are becoming more unequal by any number of measures. Is the ability to pursue happiness as unequally shared as income in the United States? While U.S. attitudes about inequality and opportunity have historically been exceptional, are they still? Do these attitudes, which are closely linked to happiness and to optimism about the future, affect individual choices about investments in the future and therefore life chances and outcomes?

This book answers these questions, using metrics and tools from the novel science of well-being measurement. It is conceptually distinct from the extensive literature on inequality and growth and from the smaller literature on measured inequality and well-being, although it clearly builds and benefits from both. The focus is the related but less studied link between well-being and attitudes about the future, and the implications of that link for the behaviors and future outcomes of different socioeconomic and demographic cohorts.

A modest body of research (including some of my own) has shown that people with more positive attitudes and/or more positive attitudes about their future mobility have higher levels of well-being, with causality running in both directions. As a result, they are more willing to invest in those futures. People with limited future opportunities have higher discount rates—meaning that they are present-biased and place less value than the average on future income, health, and other outcomes. This tends to be because they have less capacity to set aside their limited means to make such investments, and because they have less confidence that those investments will pay off (De Neve et al., 2013; De Neve and Oswald, 2012; Oswald, Proto, and Sgroi, 2009; Graham and Pettinato, 2002a, 2002b; Graham, Eggers, and Sukhtankar, 2004). The patterns across individuals and socioeconomic cohorts in these beliefs tend to be self-perpetuating, meanwhile (Lerner, 1982; Butler, 2014).

Does the increasingly unequal distribution of opportunity in the United States thus imply that disadvantaged cohorts of society are more likely to focus on the short term, at the expense of investments in their own and their children's futures? Are increasing sectors of U.S. society simply living in the moment, not as badly as Sukhov perhaps, but without the opportunities to seek better and more fulfilling lives, as James Thurlow Adams posits? How does the United States compare with other countries on this score?

Well-being metrics give us a novel tool to measure the linkages between mobility attitudes and well-being in its various dimensions. So-called hedonic metrics capture daily experience and respondents' mental states—such as happiness at the moment, stress, and anxiety—as they experience their daily lives. Evaluative metrics capture respondents' attitudes about their lives as a whole, including how they change over the life course and the ability to lead meaningful and purposeful lives. Respondents with different attitudes about the future may emphasize one or the other well-being dimension more. If capabilities and opportunities are limited, individuals focus more on the daily experience aspects of their lives and well-being, as they live from day to day without the capacity to plan for the future (Graham and Lora, 2009; Graham and Nikolova, 2013; Haushofer and Fehr, 2014). Those with more capabilities and opportunities often focus more on the longer term dimensions of their lives and well-being—such as purpose and fulfillment—even at the expense of daily quality of life, at least in the short term.

This book builds on my research on well-being and on mobility and opportunity in countries around the world. I explore the linkages between the distribution of income, attitudes about inequality and future mobility, and well-being in the United States, and also provide some comparisons with other countries and regions. This scholarship is distinct from existing work on inequality in its focus on the well-being–beliefs channel and its implications for individual choices about the future. The "Gatsby curve" in economics posits that children from different backgrounds will have even larger gaps in outcomes than their parents did, since better-off parents have more resources to invest in their children (Krueger, 2012). In this instance, we are exploring the role of beliefs, which are also passed on from parents to children, with the gap growing ever larger between children from different socioeconomic backgrounds as the differences in the opportunities and life experiences of the rich and the poor grow.

If we are an increasingly divided society now—from the perspective of both available opportunities and attitudes about what the future holds—will we be even more divided in the future? The Declaration of Independence promises the opportunity to seek life fulfillment and happiness—in its fullest sense, for all U.S. citizens. Is happiness for all an increasingly elusive dream?

Inequality: A Complex Topic

Inequality is a controversial topic. After years of being off the table, it is now front and center in political and polemical debates. It is complex to measure, and the standard metrics that are used, such as the Gini coefficient or the 90/10 ratio, while useful for economists, are difficult for the average layman or laywoman to understand. In addition, these measures provide snapshots of distributions at one point in time, and do not change much in time periods that are relevant to political or policy cycles. The measures also mask very different trends in mobility and opportunity across societies and cohorts within them. Meanwhile, the data that are necessary to measure mobility and opportunity are rare, as they entail following the same individuals or cohorts over time.

There is a vast literature on the linkages between inequality and growth, with some of the linkages being positive, and many others negative (see Salverda, Nolan, and Smeeding, 2009, and the many essays therein for a comprehensive review). Some inequality is constructive and rewards productivity and innovation; some is destructive and creates disincentives for disadvantaged cohorts to invest in their futures and in those of their children (Birdsall and Graham, 1999). These vary across and within societies, and are also affected by structural trends in the world economy, such as technology and skill-driven growth. The standard inequality measures tell us very little about these more complex phenomena.

Because it is relatively easy to measure them, most of the debate, at least among economists, has been about trends in income inequality and, less frequently, about trends in mobility over time. Yet regardless of trends in the data, the channel by which inequality has the most direct effects on individual welfare and resulting behaviors may be what it signals in different societies and among different cohorts. In other words, if inequality—and particularly the gains of those who are being successful—is a sign of hope and potential future progress to others in society, then it has positive signaling effects. Alternatively, if it is a marker of persistent advantage for some and disadvantage for others, it has negative effects. What inequality signals is, in turn, linked to behavioral outcomes, such as effort in the labor market and investments in health and education.

Studies of inequality and individual well-being—in the United States, the European Union, and Latin America—have yielded mixed results, precisely because inequality has different implications in different contexts. Albert Hirschman's well-known "tunnel hypothesis" provides a good conceptual frame for interpreting these mixed results. In a seminal article published in 1973, Hirschman described two kinds of signals and their potential effects. He compared inequality in the development process to a traffic jam in a tunnel. When one lane of traffic begins to move, initially it gives those in the other lanes reason for hope, a signal that they may also soon move forward. Yet if only that lane continues to move and the others stay stalled, then the drivers in the stalled lanes become frustrated and engage in dangerous behaviors such as jumping the median (Hirschman and Rothschild, 1973).

Partly as a result of these multiple possible meanings, there is no consistent pattern in the results of studies of inequality and life satisfaction and other measures of well-being (Alesina, Di Tella, and MacCulloch, 2004; Graham and Felton, 2006; Oishi, Kesebir, and Diener, 2011; Van Praag and Ferrer-i-Carbonell, 2009). Of the many studies that I review in Chapter 3, some find a negative correlation between inequality and life satisfaction, others a positive one, and some none at all. This is likely because there can be negative comparison effects—e.g., if those in your reference group have higher incomes you feel less well-off—or positive signaling effects, or they may both operate at the same time, depending on the context. In more stable economies, such as the United States and Europe, comparison effects seem to dominate, while in contexts of economic transition or change, inequality seems to provide a sign of positive progress (at least initially), as in the tunnel example.

The reference or peer group that individuals are comparing themselves to plays a role, as well as their belief structures. Positive signaling effects are more likely in smaller areas, such as neighborhoods and small towns, perhaps because public goods such as schools and parks are shared at this level. In contrast, in larger reference groups, such as large cities, comparison effects are more likely. In the latter instance, the large differences in wealth are quite visible, and at the same time the lives of those at the top and the bottom are much further apart from each other. Thus the "success" of the very wealthy seems much more out of reach for those at the bottom.

Belief structures about what determines "success" also matter. In contexts where the majority believes that connections or unfair advantage determine success, inequality typically has a negative relationship with life satisfaction. In those where high income gains are seen as a just reward for hard work, skills, productivity, and innovation (as used to be the case in the United States), inequality usually has a positive or at least neutral association with well-being. And, as described in subsequent chapters, individual experiences along these lines, such as being rewarded fairly or unfairly at school or in the workplace, can result in persistent belief structures about the ability to get ahead in the future.

An important question in the debates today is whether the United States' long-held reputation as a land of opportunity is still backed by exceptional rates of mobility. High levels of inequality were traditionally seen as rewards in a dynamic and fluid labor market and as a positive signal to individuals of where they might end up in the future. Material success was seen as a just reward for hard work and innovation. Yet there is now significant evidence that U.S. mobility rates—both inter- and intragenerational—are actually lower than those in many other countries in the OECD (Brunori, Ferreira, and Peragine, 2013). We know less about public perceptions of inequality in the context of these changes, and belief structures tend to lag behind objective changes. Yet the new data that I present throughout the book suggest that they have indeed changed a great deal.

Attitudes about Future Mobility

For decades U.S. citizens accepted and even supported exceptionally high rates of inequality and relatively low rates of redistributive taxation because of a widely held belief in the inequality-opportunity link (Bénabou and Ok, 2001). Bénabou and Tirole (2006), based on World Values Survey data, found that only 29 percent of Americans believed that the poor are trapped in poverty, while only 30 percent believed that luck rather than effort or education determines income. In contrast, the figures for Europeans were nearly double that—60 and 54 percent, respectively. Conversely, Americans were twice as likely as Europeans (on average) to believe that the poor "are lazy or lack willpower" (60 percent vs. 26 percent) and that "in the long run, hard work usually brings a better life" (59 percent vs. 34–43 percent).

These beliefs tend to correlate with actual levels of redistribution across countries, even though they are often out of touch with reality—as in the case of U.S. mobility rates. Bénabou and Tirole cite various studies that show that such beliefs are chosen and held on to despite what the data show about actual trends in inequality and mobility; the average individual believes that there is more mobility than there actually is. This phenomenon was described by Lerner (1982) as the "belief in a just world"—such as the nearly universal human tendency to want to believe that people generally get what they deserve.[1]

Yet these studies were based on data for the 1990s, and objective trends in inequality—and more recently awareness of them—have changed a great deal. The explosive amount of public attention given to Thomas Piketty's (2014) excellent but highly technical book on inequality in capital was an indication that attitudes might be changing, at least in some circles. The 2016 electoral debate and the remarkable support for antisystem candidates such as Bernie Sanders, promising to address the plight of those who have fallen behind, also revealed significant levels of public concern about the issue.

In addition to the high levels of concern, there is evidence that attitudes about inequality are increasingly divided across ideological lines. A recent Pew poll, for example, found that 57 percent of Republicans believed that people who became rich did so because they worked harder than others, while only 27 percent of Democrats thought the same. In contrast, only 32 percent of Republicans felt that people were poor because of circumstances beyond their control, compared to 63 percent of Democrats (Blow, 2014). Kuziemko et al. (2015), meanwhile, find that the difference between

---

[1] Their theoretical model of just beliefs brings together (1) a demand side, for motivated beliefs, resulting from imperfect willpower (or divergent parent-child preferences) and/or anticipatory feelings about this world or the next and (2) a supply side, taking the form of selective recall/awareness or that of parental indoctrination and then (3) general equilibrium interactions between individuals' cognitive choices, arising endogenously via collective policy decisions.

liberals and conservatives is the most important explanatory variable in the determinants of attitudes about inequality.

The latest Gallup data (Jones, 2015) show that a reasonably high percentage of Americans—56 percent—say that the amount of income tax they pay is fair (down from a recent high of 64 percent in 2003). Yet there are differences across groups, with lower and upper income groups displaying less support than those in the middle. And, among lower income groups, it is those who identify as Republicans who have become less likely to view their taxes as fair, while lower income Democrats have not changed their opinions. This again reflects a deep ideological divide and the fact that antigovernment sentiment is increasing in the United States (Jones, 2015).

Programs targeted to the poor tend to be stigmatized in general, and are generally believed to create dependence on government. They tend to have very little support among the broader U.S. public (Swenson, 2015; Gilens, 1999). Indeed, the functioning of these programs reflects the differential levels of public support for them. Swenson (2015) describes how the bureaucracies that support programs that provide universal benefits, such as social security and Medicare (which function like semiprivatized programs), are much more user-friendly than those for programs targeted to the poor, such as Temporary Assistance for Needy Families, food stamps, and Medicaid.

Robert Putnam (2015) describes the evolution of our social welfare system as "the privatization of risk," with the majority unwilling to support the neediest because they do not conceive of them as part of a broader social collective. Gilens's work, meanwhile, suggests that sympathy for welfare beneficiaries varies broadly depending on how racially homogenous neighborhoods are and on whether or not respondents have had friends or relatives on welfare.

Misperceptions about poverty, inequality, and mobility extend well beyond the ideological divide. Two recent psychological studies find that Americans across the economic spectrum misjudge the amount of upward mobility there is. There may be psychological utility to that: it helps the rich justify their wealth and provides hope for the poor. The studies were based on experiments where three thousand respondents were shown pictures of income quintiles and asked to estimate the likelihood that a randomly selected person born in the bottom quintile would move up to each of the others in his or her lifetime. Respondents' estimates were compared with actual trends based on Pew data. Participants overshot positive probabilities by nearly 15 percent points, and respondents with less than a college education were more likely to overshoot. Responses to questions about how many college students come from families in the bottom 20 percent of the income bracket demonstrated similar bias. The respondents thought that the poorest attend college at a rate five times more than they actually do as shown in the Current Population Survey data (Kraus, Davidai, and Nussbaum, 2015).

There are more puzzles about who supports redistribution, as shown by two recent studies (Ashok, Kuziemko, and Washington, 2015; Kuziemko et al., 2015). While support is increasing among some cohorts, it is falling significantly among the elderly and blacks. For the elderly, trends are in part linked to the extent to which Medicare and its bureaucracy has been disassociated from the government. Rather remarkably, 40 percent of Medicare recipients do not think they receive support from a government medical insurance program! For blacks, it may be due to the narrowing of wage differentials, although that has stalled somewhat in recent years. Blacks are more likely than whites to say that people get ahead due to luck rather than hard work, but that differential has narrowed in the past decade. Those blacks who believe it is luck rather than hard work, meanwhile, are more supportive of redistribution. I discuss my research findings on high levels of optimism for the future among blacks—and particularly poor blacks compared to poor whites—as well as how the findings are related to the above trends in Chapter 4.

More generally, my research finds stark differences in attitudes about the future—and in beliefs about the value of hard work in particular—across rich and poor cohorts in the United States. Indeed the gaps are much greater than they are in Latin America, on average. Rather remarkably, belief that hard work will pay off in the future among the U.S. poor is significantly lower than among the poor in Latin America and the Caribbean (LAC), while the rich in the United States score much higher on hard work beliefs than do the rich in LAC. This may be an example of Lerner's beliefs in a just world explanation.

The available data show that public confidence in the American Dream/U.S. exceptionalism is not what it is reputed to be. My research highlights clear markers between low-income cohorts living at the moment with little faith in or ability to invest in the future and wealthy cohorts who believe in and make major investments in their own and their children's futures. The outcomes of the latter cohorts—in the wealth, health, and life fulfillment arenas—are further and further away from the realities lived by those at the bottom.

It is difficult to establish a direction of causality, as beliefs and behaviors seem to interact and often become self-fulfilling prophesies. Even so, these growing differences coincide with and perhaps cause our increasing inability to conceive of societal welfare as a collective responsibility. The tattered support for extending health insurance to the millions of uninsured is one marker of this. The huge division in attitudes about the causes of poverty is another. An increase in mortality rates among uneducated whites, driven by suicides, drug addiction, and other self-destructive behaviors, signaling desperation, is perhaps the most troubling marker of all.

Well-Being Dimensions and Metrics

While it is not easy to measure the effects of inequality on individual welfare, well-being metrics provide a promising tool. The relatively new science of well-being has developed into an increasingly accepted approach in economics and in the social sciences more generally. The metrics are particularly useful for exploring questions that revealed preferences (e.g., analysis based on data that measure consumption and other choices within a fixed budget constraint) do not provide good answers to, such as in situations where respondents do not have the capacity to reveal a preference or because their behaviors are driven not by rational or optimal choices, but rather by norms, addiction, or self-control problems. Such questions include the welfare effects of macro and institutional arrangements that individuals are powerless to change, with inequality a prime example, and of strong normative arrangements, such as discrimination and/or caste systems, and of behavioral choices such as excessive smoking and/or obesity.

The most recent research makes clear distinctions between two well-being dimensions mentioned earlier: evaluative—how people think of their lives as a whole—and hedonic—capturing how people experience their daily lives (Stone and Mackie, 2013; Graham and Nikolova, 2015). Individuals with higher levels of evaluative well-being have more of a sense of what their futures look like and thus are more likely and more able to delay gratification today to make investments in those futures. Individuals with less agency or capacity to craft their futures (and lower prospects of upward mobility) may focus more on the daily experience dimension of well-being precisely because their future outlooks are far less certain and within their sphere of influence.

These distinctions complement Sen's well-known capabilities approach, but from the perspective of well-being. I define "agency" here as the capacity to pursue a purposeful and fulfilling life (Graham, 2011b) and "capabilities" as "the freedom to achieve various lifestyles," which in turn requires having the means (both material and emotional) to do so (Sen, 1984).

Another important and related dimension of well-being, which we know less about, is eudemonia—the extent to which people have purpose or meaning in their lives. It is implicitly captured in evaluative well-being metrics. There are some new efforts under way to measure it explicitly, including in the well-being modules of the British Office of National Statistics, using a question that asks respondents the extent to which they feel that the things they do in their lives are worthwhile (Adler, Dolan, and Kavetsos, 2014; Office of National Statistics, 2015). Not surprisingly, eudemonic well-being tracks more closely with life satisfaction, the evaluative metric, than with the hedonic metrics. Whether or not people have the capacity to lead fulfilling and purposeful lives—and how that is linked to their future outlooks and discount rates—is an important theme in this book.

The scientific analysis of these issues has now developed to a point that scholars are also able to tease out causal channels related to different dimensions of well-being and related attitudes. One suggestive set of findings, noted above, is that individuals with higher levels of well-being (on average) tend to also have higher prospects of upward mobility and, as a result, invest more in their own and in their children's future, investments that are in turn reflected in better labor market and health outcomes (Graham, Eggers, and Sukhtankar, 2004; De Neve and Oswald, 2012; De Neve et al., 2013). What is less well understood is how this actually works.

Work in the field of experimental economics suggests an important role for positive emotions, such as optimism, in inspiring effort and productivity (Oswald, Proto, and Sgroi, 2009). Psychologists have shown that positive emotion influences self-control and performance, as well as the capacities of choice and innovative content, memory recall, and tendency toward altruism

(Isen, 2000; Isen et al., 1978). Both bodies of work, while at an early stage in their development, suggest there is a role for intrinsic versus external motivation—in other words effort that is driven by individuals' own motivation to achieve certain goals rather than by the need for external rewards or validation (see also Bénabou and Tirole, 2003). Recent work on well-being in the United States by Kahneman and Deaton (2010) shows that while emotional well-being is correlated with income up to median levels of income, below which day-to-day living is often a struggle, emotional well-being no longer correlates with income once those levels are surpassed. Thus after a certain point, more income does not "buy" positive emotions, but insufficient income is more likely to result in negative ones.

In Chapter 4, I also look at the role of negative daily experience, such as chronic health problems, pain, anger, and stress, all of which are starkly divided across rich and poor cohorts in the United States. Poor cohorts are much more likely to be concerned about daily existence, stress, and struggles, and less able to think about or plan for the future. The rich have much higher levels of evaluative well-being, in large part because they can envision and plan for their future lives. I also look at the extent to which inequality plays a mediating role, and find differences depending on the local distribution of income.

Psychologists define stress as a feeling of strain or pressure. Humans perceive stress when they do not believe that they have the resources to cope with the obstacles facing them. Small amounts of stress can be beneficial and play a positive motivating role, as in athletic performance or reacting to the environment (Schneiderman, Ironson, and Siegel, 2005). Yet excessive stress can result in increased risks of harmful conditions, such as heart attacks, strokes, and depression. I explore these differences in Chapter 4, including the extent to which there are different kinds of stress across cohorts, with "good" stress associated with goal achievement and related challenges and "bad" stress associated with daily struggles and circumstances beyond individuals' control.

A related trend is new evidence that inequality in life satisfaction in the United States has increased recently. Life satisfaction typically becomes more equal as countries grow wealthier (in per capita GDP terms). This leveling off is usually driven by trends at the bottom of the distribution—for example, there are fewer respondents with very low levels of life satisfaction, as the numbers of the very poor living precarious existences fall. The United States fit this trend for several decades, but there is some new evidence that this has now changed with inequality in life satisfaction increasing in the past five or so years (Stevenson and Wolfers, 2008; Clark, Fleche, and Senik, 2016; Helliwell, Layard, and Sachs, 2013; Goff, Helliwell, and Mayraz, 2016).

Our initial analysis of the Gallup Daily U.S. data for 2008 to the present suggests that inequality in life satisfaction increased at the time of the 2009 financial crisis—a time when, not surprisingly, average life satisfaction was also falling markedly (Graham, Chattopadhyay, and Picon, 2010a). This increase was probably driven by an increase in low scores at the bottom of the well-being distribution as the number of vulnerable individuals—including the long-term unemployed—grew. These same cohorts also benefited disproportionately less from the recovery.

Another related but distinct trend is that although the relationship between life satisfaction and per capita GDP levels is typically positive, the relationship with economic growth (e.g., changes) is more mixed and contested. Indeed, the relationship between life satisfaction and growth tends to be negative during periods of very rapid growth, as in China in the 1990s and Korea several decades earlier (Graham and Lora, 2009), and is often associated with increases in inequality and insecurity as rewards to different skill sets change. This could plausibly be a factor in the trends observed in the United States in the recent decades, not least because those who are falling behind typically do not have the skills and education necessary to succeed in an increasingly skills-driven economy.

There are currently many efforts under way to incorporate well-being metrics into the official statistics that are collected by governments around the world. This would allow scholars and policy makers to track trends in well-being (or ill-being) across cohorts within countries and across countries over time, as a complement to the metrics that are already in GNP data. The British government began to include these metrics in its national statistics in 2012, and the OECD has issued guidelines for best practice for statistics offices around the world interested in doing so. Even the U.S. Committee on National Statistics has entered into this discussion, as a response to a National Academy of Sciences panel report on well-being metrics and policy, and well-being metrics are currently included in a number of U.S. surveys.[2]

---

[2] I served on this panel. For the full report, see http://www.nap.edu/catalog.php?record_id=18548.

As I note in Chapters 5 and 6, tracking well-being trends in a consistent and timely manner would allow us to better understand some of the worrisome pockets of ill-being and desperation that are described later in the book, and possibly help prevent some of their worst manifestations. Better understanding of variance in well-being (across its many dimensions) among different cohorts, and why some maintain hope for the future and make related investments and others do not, might also provide new insights into how to improve policy in the future.

Well-Being, Beliefs, and Behavior

The proposition that people's beliefs and hopes about the future influence behaviors and outcomes stems from my own past research linking well-being to future outcomes in the income and health arenas (Graham, Eggers, and Sukhtankar, 2004; Graham and Pettinato, 2002b), and, more importantly, from new research by others that explores the links between well-being and future outcomes across a wider range of areas (De Neve et al., 2013; De Neve and Oswald, 2012).

This relationship between beliefs and behaviors and its implications for the outcomes of future generations is one of the most important themes in the book, and yet the one that we know the least about. There are many empirical and experimental studies that highlight its existence, but there are still unanswered questions about when and how it operates, as well as about the direction of causality. Causality could run in two directions. While experiencing inequality and injustice may reduce individuals' confidence in their ability to get ahead in the future (and thus how much they are willing to invest in the future), individuals who are innately less happy (e.g., due to genes or repeated negative shocks in the past) and less confident may be more upset by awareness of inequality and/or less able to rebound from negative experiences.

Despite all of these unanswered questions, there is a growing body of work that highlights this channel from beliefs to behaviors and its important role. Experimental work based on interventions that increase optimism is suggestive of the direction of causality, even if it cannot fully account for the role of innate differences in character traits. For example, Jeff Butler's (2014) research shows that introducing salient—i.e., visible—inequality affects people's beliefs about their own ability rather than the effort they put into things. Individuals who are in an artificially constructed low pay group in his experiments put forth more effort and perform about on par as those in the artificially constructed high pay group (and actually higher in the tasks that were based on effort rather than ability), but salient inequality—e.g., being told that they are earning less—affects their beliefs about their ability.

Hoxby and Avery (2012) find that even when offered a free college education, high-ability disadvantaged students tend to choose less prestigious rather than more competitive schools. Disadvantage itself seems to diminish prospective students' assessments of the value of attending college if they believe that they cannot compete with students from more privileged backgrounds; they may also have less information about what constitutes a good school at the same time. The colleges simply seem beyond their reach. Along the same lines, social psychologist Daphna Oyserman (2013) has researched how students' identity affects how they perceive "impossible" versus "important" tasks and how they feel they rank on those tasks. She has found that when prompted about their identity as minorities prior to undertaking particular tasks, high school students were more likely to perceive the tasks as "impossible" than when they were not.

These differences in both real and perceived ability can begin very early on in the life cycle. Psychologists Betty Hart and Todd Risley (1995) in the United States in the 1990s found that there were "intractable differences in rates of vocabulary growth" depending on socioeconomic status because of the kinds of words—and exposure to positive versus negative words—that the children of different socioeconomic cohorts received.[3] There are many other examples and studies, many of which are reviewed in greater detail in Chapter 5.

Throughout the book, I incorporate the more recent research that explores the distinct well-being dimensions and I use these metrics as a lens into the very different lives and future outlooks that are depicted in the above studies. Individuals with higher levels of evaluative well-being, for example, who have more of a sense of what their futures look like and more capacity to craft those futures may experience lower levels of hedonic well-being (such

---

[3] For a more complete review of this literature, see Meerman (2009).

as more stress) as they work to make investments in those futures. Individuals with less agency or capacity to craft their futures (and lower prospects of upward mobility for example) may focus more on the daily experience dimension of well-being precisely because their future outlooks are far less certain. The effects of the stress that they experience, typically associated with circumstances that they cannot control, are very different, as discussed in Chapter 4.

Research based on experiments on the benefits of programs that transfer income to poor individuals in Kenya finds that the stress associated with living day to day contributes to shortsighted and risk-averse decision making. Stress may limit attention, resulting in an emphasis on habitual behaviors at the expense of goal-oriented ones (Haushofer and Fehr, 2014). Similarly, Eduardo Lora and I (Graham and Lora, 2009) find in Latin America that the most important variable to the well-being of the poor, after having enough food to eat, is friends and family whom they can rely on in times of need, while the most important variables to the well-being of the rich are work and health. Friends and family are critical safety nets in the day-to-day survival challenges faced by the poor, while work and health are the things that give respondents with more means the capacity to make choices about the kinds of lives that they want to lead.

A consistent trend that emerges from well-being metrics and reflects these different time horizons is something that I identified years ago: the happy peasant and frustrated achiever paradox, which provides a micro-level mirror into the paradox of unhappy growth. In data from around the world—such as Peru, Russia, and China—I have found that poor people with very little or no income mobility will report to be happy, while respondents who have recently made income gains and exited poverty report to be unhappy and frustrated with their economic situations (Graham and Pettinato, 2002a). In part this can be explained by the rising aspirations, new awareness, and uncertainty that often accompany the economic development process. But it is also explained by what dimension of well-being respondents are emphasizing as they answer these questions. The very poorest typically focus on the daily experience dimension of well-being, as they do not have the luxury of thinking about longer time horizons.

This contrasts strongly with the perspective of those with greater capabilities and life choices. Thus when respondents with more means are asked about their own lives and well-being, they are more likely to think about their lives as a whole—the evaluative dimension. This difference shows up in the data when specific questions pertaining to each dimension are included. The above-cited Kahneman and Deaton (2010) work shows that not having enough means is bad for both dimensions of well-being, but after a certain point more money does not make daily experience better. More money does not make a long commute less annoying or time with friends more pleasurable, for example. In contrast, the correlation between income and evaluative well-being continues up to the highest levels of income. This is because people with more income have a greater capacity to lead the kinds of lives that they desire.

Some of our newest work, which is based on where respondents are in the well-being distribution and their associated behaviors, confirms this generally positive link between well-being, health, and productivity, on average. Yet we also find that respondents at the very top end of the well-being distribution (e.g., the happiest) diverge a bit, and value full-time employment and income less than the average, but learning and creativity more (Graham and Nikolova, 2015), while the least happy respondents are more likely to value money. The likelihood of being in this top well-being quantile, meanwhile, and having the luxury to choose between more creative and meaningful pursuits, which may yield less income, hinges to some extent on having sufficient means. Happier respondents also tend to have more happy life years (Graham and Ruiz-Pozuelo, 2016).

Nickerson and colleagues (2003)—in "The Dark Side of the American Dream"—use panel data for college students and find that having financial success as an important goal early in life is, on average, negatively correlated with life satisfaction later on. They also find that the negative effect of valuing financial success is much worse for those who start at lower levels of household income, who will have a more difficult time achieving it. Thus while the least happy value material/pecuniary dimensions of life more, there seems to be a doubly negative effect of being poor and in this category.

Respondents with higher levels of well-being also seem to have more resilience when they experience negative shocks like unemployment. Martin Binder and Alexander Coad (2015) find that those respondents in the highest well-being/life satisfaction quantile suffer about one-third the well-being costs of being unemployed than do those in the least happy quantile (e.g., the latter suffer greater losses in well-being). They also find distinct differences when they use markers of mental health rather than life satisfaction. Those in the lowest mental health category suffer twice as much from being unemployed than do those in the best off category. In contrast, the highest mental well-being categories do not differ from each other as much from the lowest as do the highest and lowest life satisfaction categories (a one-half difference in the former case and a two-thirds difference in the latter).

As such, and as psychologists are careful to explain, negative affect/moods and depression are not the direct analogue to high levels of life satisfaction. In other words, depression and happiness are not one construct that can be measured on a continuous scale. The depressed have distinct negative traits, and the happiest have distinct positive ones. How the traits of those with the highest and lowest levels of well-being (e.g., those at the tails of the well-being distribution) interact with behaviors is one of the questions in this book. Most of the research in this area is exploratory rather than definitive, but has the potential to contribute to the debate on heredity versus the environment in determining individual behaviors and outcomes.

The very different time horizons and life prospects that people with different means and opportunities have is a key theme in this book and in the channel from beliefs to behaviors more generally. Indeed, making clear distinctions between these two dimensions and how they vary across respondents in different situations and with different capabilities is one way to bridge the gap between well-being as measured by the capabilities approach famously introduced by Amartya Sen (1984) and well-being as assessed by self-reports. Sen's early critiques of the happiness literature focused on the "happy slaves"—those respondents in compromised situations with low expectations who reported to be very happy because they had adapted to their situation, as in the case of the happy peasants and frustrated achievers paradox mentioned above.

The capabilities approach assumes that welfare hinges on an individual's capability to achieve certain key functionings (such as being nourished and avoiding premature mortality) and having the agency or autonomy to decide what he or she wants to achieve. Binder (2014) suggests exploring how different well-being dimensions vary across people, as well as assessing how the value respondents attach to certain functionings changes over time. The importance of income or nourishment matters may also change as individuals achieve the capability to pursue other dimensions of well-being, such as purposefulness, and at the same time it will also vary depending on where in the well-being distribution individuals are, that is, how much food or money they already have.

The framework introduced in this book complements these lines of thinking, and hinges on the capacity of individuals to experience both dimensions of well-being, thereby having the capabilities and the agency to seek life fulfillment if they want or choose to do so. Individuals who are compromised in their expectations, due to limited education, poverty, or other constraints, primarily experience the hedonic dimension—either because daily living is a struggle or because of limited expectations and time horizons they have lower levels of overall well-being within this frame and are also less likely to invest in their future outcomes. The capacity to experience well-being in its fullest sense, therefore, is often closely linked to an individual's position in the income distribution, and this is especially true in the United States today.

In the next chapter of the book I review trends in inequality and mobility in the United States over the past few decades, and how those compare with what has happened in other countries, particularly but not exclusively in OECD countries. Chapter 3 then goes on to ask who still believes in the American Dream. It begins with a review of what we know about the relationship between inequality, well-being, and attitudes about future mobility. It summarizes what we know from survey data on attitudes about inequality and opportunity in the United States, and then places those attitudes in the context of those in other countries and regions, based on our new data and analysis with a focus on individuals' beliefs in the role of hard work in future success.

Chapter 4 focuses on what it means to be poor in the United States and how poverty affects expectations about the future. I explore patterns in optimism across different racial and socioeconomic cohorts. I find surprising differences, for example, with poor blacks and Hispanics (particularly the former) being much more optimistic about the future than poor whites. These differential levels of optimism can result in very different discount rates across individuals, with those with less faith in the future far more likely to live in the moment, focused on the day to day, and less likely to make investments in their own and their children's future. The most vivid example of these differential levels of optimism—and the extreme desperation among some cohorts—is the increase in mortality rates due to preventable causes such as suicide and opioid addiction. Increasing support for populist and nativist politicians with unrealistic promises among the same cohorts is another manifestation.

I also examine the extent to which these patterns are mediated by stress and inequality. Stress that is associated with constant uncertainty and circumstances beyond individuals' control, which characterizes the lives of many of the poor, is particularly deleterious to well-being. It erodes individuals' capacity to plan ahead, as is highlighted in the well-known research of Sendhil Mullainathan and Eldar Shafir (2013). High levels of inequality, meanwhile, which make success seem out of reach, can contribute to lack of faith in the future among those at the bottom of the distribution.

Chapter 5 reviews the nascent research on the linkages between well-being, optimism about the future, and behavioral outcomes of interest in the health, wealth, and social arenas, among others. It discusses the implications of the beliefs and behaviors channel for the children of cohorts with different beliefs and thus for intergenerational patterns in inequality and opportunity. I also discuss my new research in progress, which aims to further tease out the direction of causality in the beliefs and behaviors channel, as well as to test the extent to which aspirations can be shifted via interventions as a means to break vicious cycles.

Finally, in Chapter 6 I offer some modest suggestions for policies that might begin to revive the fragile American Dream. I also highlight the role that well-being metrics and markers can play in identifying negative beliefs and behaviors channels before they result in the kinds of desperate outcomes that are described in the book, such as rising mortality rates. The metrics can also play a role in informing and assessing policy interventions going forward.

A Note on Data

I rely on a number of extensive data sets of well-being, both for the United States and around the world, and examine the link between attitudes about inequality/future mobility and well-being. I examine U.S. trends in comparative perspective, both with those in other countries in the OECD and with trends in countries in Latin America, where despite traditionally high levels of inequality, rates are gradually falling and rates of mobility are concurrently rising.

I use detailed individual-level data for the United States (the Gallup Healthways data) as well as worldwide data (the Gallup World Poll and the Latinobarómetro, among others).[4] Unfortunately, the larger worldwide data sets are cross-section rather than panel, which makes it much more difficult to explicitly explore how attitudes about inequality and mobility link to behavioral outcomes of interest, such as investments in the labor markets and education. Going forward, I am planning to explore these questions, in collaboration with several others, in country-level panel data sets for the United States and Latin America, as well as via experiments in smaller scale surveys (discussed in Chapter 5).

[4] I am a Senior Scientist at Gallup and, as such, have access to the Gallup data sets.

CHAPTER 2

What Happened to Horatio Alger?

U.S. Trends in Inequality and Opportunity in Comparative Perspective

You have pleaded the cause of social justice and the right of the individual to happiness through economic security, a living wage, and an opportunity to share in things that enrich and ennoble human life.

—F. D. Roosevelt in a letter to historian John Ryan, May 25, 1939[1]

The Problem of Measurement; or, Measuring Like for Like?

Historically, the American Dream—and the conceptualization of the average U.S. citizen—focused on equality of opportunities rather than equality of outcomes, based on the principle that if people are provided with equal opportunities, then differences in outcomes must reflect individual effort. Horatio Alger, the nineteenth-century author, wrote numerous novels about impoverished boys and their rise from humble backgrounds to lives of middle-class security and comfort through hard work, determination, courage, and honesty. His stories of these young Americans rising from rags to riches became emblematic of the American Dream.

Yet that may not always be the case, as there are large differences in the endowments that people inherit (in terms of both physical assets and human capital). As such the opportunities available to all may not be as equal as they seem, as those with inferior endowments have less capacity to take them up.

---

[1] I am grateful to Don Stabile of St. Mary's College for finding this quotation for me.

John Roemer (1993) characterized these differences in the form of a birth lottery, in which some people had much better luck than others. His strategy for equalizing opportunity would compensate people for bad luck in the birth lottery, but still hold them responsible for their choices and effort. As this chapter and subsequent chapters highlight, the reality in the United States today is very far from this idea.

Indeed one of the most prevalent questions in the debates today is whether the United States' long-held reputation as a land of opportunity is still backed by exceptional rates of mobility. Its high levels of inequality were traditionally seen as rewards in a dynamic and fluid labor market and a positive signal to individuals of where they might end up in the future. Yet there is now significant evidence that this is no longer the case, and that mobility rates—both inter- and intragenerational—are actually lower than those in many other countries in the OECD. There is still little consensus on this question, however, in part due to the complexity of the underlying concepts and metrics.

Inequality is a complex topic. The metrics that are used to measure it are difficult for the average layperson to understand. In addition and more importantly, inequality has many distinct facets that can matter differently to different people. Economists tend to measure and worry about relative differences: the extent to which there are changes in the proportional shares of the total distribution held by different groups. Discussions in the media and elsewhere tend to focus on absolute differences in the shares held by different cohorts. These two facets of inequality do not always match each other. For example, an income increase that doubles the incomes of two individuals, one who began with $100 and the other with $1,000, increases the absolute difference between them, from $900 to $1,800, but the proportional share of each in the total distribution has not changed.

A key issue for this discussion is how inequality in income (whether absolute or proportional) links to intra- and intergenerational income mobility. The Gatsby curve posits that if these gaps are sufficiently large, as they are in the United States today, then the odds of the children born at the bottom end of the distribution advancing to the top are much lower, as the advantages that the children at the top receive from their parents—such as access to better schools, a wide range of extracurricular activities, and travel and other opportunities—are much greater than the ones available to those at

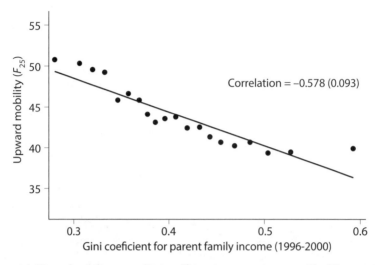

Figure 2.1. Upward mobility versus Gini coefficient in commuting zones. The "Great Gatsby" curve within the United States.

Source: Chetty et al. (2014).

Note: Data for each commuting zone (or narrow geographic area) are grouped into 20 bins based on the Gini coefficient for parents' family income, which is shown along the horizontal axis. The vertical axis shows the average percentile rank for a child born at the 25th percentile of the family income distribution in a commuting zone with a Gini coefficient that falls within the bin indicated by the horizontal axis.

the bottom. Even worse, children at the bottom often experience significant disadvantages, such as a greater likelihood of having dysfunctional families and/or growing up in violent neighborhoods (see Figure 2.1). A wealth of empirical evidence, discussed in this and subsequent chapters, supports the Gatsby curve hypothesis. I explicitly explore whether there is also a Gatsby curve in attitudes about the future in Chapter 4.

There is also much debate in economics on the effects of inequality on individual well-being. In part this is because there is no consensus on how inequality affects well-being.[2] The channels range from concerns about relative differences (which, as noted above, economists worry about) or absolute differences (which people tend to worry about), to the effects of transitory

---

[2] Well-being is defined here as the income and nonincome determinants of human welfare; its two distinct dimensions and the metrics used to measure it are described in Chapter 1.

changes in the distribution, to long-term differences in opportunities that are transmitted across generations, among others. The average citizen may not notice inequality at all unless there are significant changes in the distribution, and these changes could as easily be at the local or firm level as at the national level.

A simple comparison between the United States and Scandinavian countries such as Sweden, Norway, and Denmark provides an example of the many possible channels. Average well-being levels are slightly higher in the Scandinavian countries, while average per capita income is slightly higher in the United States. Inequality could affect well-being in the United States simply because there are more people with lower levels of absolute income and a small number of individuals with incomes that are far above the average.[3] This result would have nothing to do with relative income differences. Alternatively, people may be more bothered by relative income differences than they are by absolute differences, and thus prefer a stagnant economy with more equality than a rapidly growing one in which there are larger absolute income differentials. There is some evidence (reviewed later in Chapter 3) that these preferences vary across societies. And social and political institutions both reflect those preferences and play a mediating role: people may be more tolerant of lower average levels of income in contexts where safety nets and social welfare benefits are more generous (as in Scandinavia versus the United States).

What inequality signals to people, meanwhile, may be quite different in advanced economies where changes are often the result of long-term demographic changes or of revisions in reward structures due to skill-driven growth, and in rapidly growing developing countries, where some cohorts often benefit before others as economies modernize and integrate into the global economy.

In addition to the conceptual complexities, the metrics that are utilized to measure inequality can make a big difference to the conclusions that are drawn (Milanovic, 2005, 2016; Burtless, 2009; Piketty and Saez, 2003; Birdsall, Ross, and Sabot, 1995; Birdsall, Graham, and Sabot, 1998; Alesina, Di

---

[3] Thus even if average per capita income is higher in the United States than Sweden, there are more people with lower absolute incomes in the United States precisely because inequality is higher and the distance between mean and median incomes is larger.

Tella, and MacCulloch, 2004). For example, conclusions about inequality trends across countries in recent decades have depended a great deal on how we account for two very large, fast-growing countries: India and China. Weighting for population size accounts for the dramatic increases in incomes and reductions in poverty in these two countries, and, as such, the worldwide distribution of income across countries is converging. Without population weights, however, and simply treating each individual country as one observation, the worldwide distribution is diverging. This is because a number of very small and very poor countries, primarily in sub-Saharan Africa, are falling way behind the rest of the world (Milanovic, 2005).[4]

Within countries, very different conclusions can be drawn about inequality trends depending on the data that are available. Because incomes at the top of the distribution are typically underreported, measures of inequality based on household surveys tend to underestimate inequality. Data based on income tax returns are better at capturing trends at the top of the distribution. Yet they lack information on the poorest individuals, who do not pay taxes, as well as on the assets of very wealthy individuals. And, in general, such data are not publicly available in many countries (nor are they always reliable). Another important problem for most countries, including the United States, is that tax return data include information only on income that is taxable, thus excluding a great deal of both government transfer benefits (which are often untaxed) and private labor income (health benefits, pension contributions) and capital income (unrealized capital gains). As such, taxable income excludes the possibly important redistributive effects of the tax system itself. Trends for the same country can thus look quite different depending on the source of data.

Countries also vary a great deal in terms of the generosity of social welfare systems, and their metrics of inequality will look very different if these transfers are accounted for (or not). Finally, while most measured inequality is vertical—for example, across individuals over an entire distribution, there are also horizontal inequalities, which are differences in outcomes across in-

---

[4]While several countries in sub-Saharan Africa had very good economic performance in the 2000–2012 time period, there are still a sufficient number of failing states and/or stagnant economies, which, when given equal weight compared to China or India, for example, drive the dispersion in the worldwide distribution.

dividuals within the same education or skill cohort as a result of divergent economic trends. Despite the focus of economists on vertical inequality, horizontal inequality may be what people notice most (Ravallion, 2004). Most people are more aware of inequalities with their counterparts at work or in their neighborhoods, for example, than they are of how they compare in the entire national-level income distribution.

What inequality signals is even more difficult to measure. Yet the signals are possibly more important to individual welfare than are measured trends. In some societies, inequality is a sign of rewards to productivity and innovation—"constructive inequality." In others, it is a sign of persistent advantages for some groups and disadvantage for others—"destructive inequality." This latter kind of inequality creates disincentives for disadvantaged cohorts, who have low prospects of upward mobility, to save and invest in the future (Birdsall and Graham, 1999).

Scholars have begun to distinguish (and measure) "unfair" and "acceptable" inequalities. The former are due to circumstances beyond individual control (such as traits inherited in Roemer's birth lottery), while those due to factors that hinge on individual responsibility, such as effort (to the extent that it is measurable), are considered "fair" (Brunori, Ferreira, and Peragine, 2013). These categories capture, roughly, the difference between inequality of opportunities and inequality of outcomes. Behavioral economists have demonstrated that notions of fairness and justice affect individual choices and have found significant deviations from the behaviors predicted by models based on the assumption of purely self-interested preferences (Fehr and Schmidt, 1999; Butler, 2014).

People's perceptions about inequality are not always in line with the actual trends, meanwhile, in part because most metrics of inequality are fairly intractable for the average layperson, and in part because attitudes are sticky and tend to lag behind actual changes in the distribution. The United States, for example, now has the highest level of inequality among OECD economies, with the exception of Mexico, and mobility rates among the lowest in this group (at least of those countries for which we have good longitudinal data). Yet, at least until very recently, these trends coexisted with a significant part of the public continuing to see inequality as a reward for individual effort in a context of exceptional rates of income mobility (Bénabou and Ok, 2001; Alesina, Di Tella, and MacCulloch, 2004).

Latin America, in contrast, has historically had much lower rates of mobility than the United States. Yet in the past two decades mobility rates have increased, poverty has fallen markedly, and even inequality has been reduced in several key countries in the region (Lustig, Pessino, and Scott, 2013).[5] Still, until recently, most of the public perceived inequality as a sign of persistent advantage for the wealthy and of disadvantage for the poor (Graham and Felton, 2006). That has indeed changed in recent years, with the gaps between the attitudes of the rich and the poor on the topic narrowing (discussed in Chapters 3 and 4).

These attitudes can and do change, but there is substantial hysteresis, which is defined as "stickiness," in factors such as prices or wages, which results in them not responding to incentives as predicted. A classic example is that of wage rates; they often do not respond to significant declines in demand or productivity in some industries, due to the bargaining power of unions or other institutional factors that make change difficult (and protect workers, at least in the short term). In an analogous sense, attitudes about inequality are also "sticky," as they are linked to deeply held beliefs and social norms that do not change easily.

Individual and societal perceptions hinge on what inequality signals. If it signals opportunity in a society where the majority of citizens possess the agency and capabilities to take up those opportunities, then it has very different effects on well-being than if it signals limited advantages for a privileged few.[6] Norms and adaptation also mediate the effects of inequality on well-being. My research finds that individuals who are accustomed to poor norms of health or high levels of crime and corruption tend to adapt their expectations downward, and report lower well-being losses from those phenomena than respondents with higher expectations (Graham, 2011a). High and persistent levels of inequality seem to play out the same way until there are very visible changes or particular events that focus public attention.

---

[5] Still, as in the case of the United States, the rare and recent studies based on tax data for Latin America (in Chile and Colombia) find persistent top-driven inequality (between the top 1 percent and the rest of the distribution). For Colombia, see Alvaredo and Londono Veliz (2013); and for Chile, see López, Figueroa, and Gutiérrez (2013).

[6] "Agency" suggests a person's capacity to pursue a fulfilling life and the opportunities to exercise choice (Graham, 2011b). For a discussion of the links between agency and capabilities and well-being more generally, see Graham and Nikolova (2015).

While individuals seem to be able to adapt to unpleasant certainty, such as high levels of crime and corruption, they are much less able to adapt to change and uncertainty, even that which is associated with progress (Graham, Chattopadhyay, and Picon, 2010a). Eduardo Lora and I have found a "paradox of unhappy growth," where, controlling for levels of GDP, which are positively associated with well-being, respondents in countries with higher rates of growth are, on average, less happy (Graham and Lora, 2009). This finding is driven by rapidly growing middle-income developing countries, where high rates of growth are, typically, associated with increasing inequality and with uncertainty as rewards to skills are changing. Rather ironically, while people seem to be able to tolerate high and persistent levels of inequality when they are static, they are bothered more by changes in the distribution, even when the changes are associated with economic progress. This seems particularly important if they do not perceive that they are benefiting from that progress, as in the example of Hirschman's tunnel mentioned in Chapter 1.

In the context of today's globalized world, some of the most notable increases in inequality (both absolute as perceived by the average citizen and relative as measured by economists) are in contexts of change and transition, even if the changes are associated with drops in extreme poverty. The major decreases in life satisfaction in the context of record levels of economic growth in China in the 1990s are a case in point. There were marked differences in gains within villages and between rural and urban areas at a time when poverty was falling at unprecedented rates (Easterlin et al., 2012; Graham, Zhou, and Zhang, 2015). The well-being effects of distributional changes in advanced developed economies like the United States, meanwhile, which are driven by structural economic changes (such as technology and skill-driven growth) and gradual demographic change, may play out quite differently, not least as they are less noticeable to the public. Yet the latter may have more lasting effects on the distribution of opportunities in the long term, as in the case of the United States.

Since the time of the U.S. financial crisis, inequality has gradually begun to enter the public debate as a serious issue; attention was then heightened by the political debates leading up to the 2016 election. Even so, concerns (or lack thereof) have been divided along ideological lines. Some scholars highlight the corrosive effects of inequality in a range of areas including concentration of political power, the increased prevalence of poverty, linkages to increased macroeconomic stability, and increasing expenditure on "positional" goods.[7] Critics label concerns about inequality as politically driven and a masked attempt to increase taxes on the wealthy. Polarization on the issue is one of the many features of the divided political debate in the United States.[8]

Trends in U.S. Inequality in Comparative Perspective

There is no doubt that inequality in the United States has increased dramatically in recent decades, both over time and in comparison to other countries in the OECD. This holds regardless of what measure of inequality is used: pre- or posttax income, Gini coefficients or income quintile shares, and/or growth in income across quintiles.

The Gini coefficient is the most common measure of income inequality, and is notionally based on a comparison of a society where one individual holds all the wealth and another where incomes are distributed completely equally. The coefficient runs from 0 to 1, with the most equal society having a coefficient of 0 and the least equal a coefficient of 1. Most countries fall in a range of coefficients between 0.25 and 0.55 (which reflects unusually high levels of inequality).

According to the Congressional Budget Office, which uses pre- and post-tax market income, the pretax Gini coefficient in the United States went from 0.48 in 1979 to 0.59 in 2007, while the posttax Gini coefficient went

---

[7] While the evidence on macroeconomic instability and inequality is rather new and arguably controversial, there is much work on the micro-level effects of inequality on worker morale and productivity, and on individual decisions about savings and investing in the future (Dadush et al., 2012; Krueger, 2012; Frank, 2011; Birdsall, Ross, and Sabot, 1995). The evidence on the effects of inequality on political representation, meanwhile, is more mixed. A recent study of how well constituent interests are represented based on data from ballot propositions in California found that rather than richer voters being better represented, as is often claimed, representation by income varies by legislator party. Republican legislators more often vote the will of their higher income constituents over those of lower income ones, and Democrats do the reverse. See Brunner, Ross, and Washington (2013).

[8] For example, the same Gallup 2011 poll reported that the percentage of Americans who feel that there is not much opportunity has gone up from 17 percent in 1998 to 41 percent in 2011, and at the same time reported that just 1 percent of respondents said inequality was America's most important problem, ranking well below issues such as "respecting each other" and "foreign aid." The first result is reported in Dadush et al. (2012), and the second in Winship (2013).

Table 2.1. Inequality in the United States: Gini coefficients for 1979 versus 2007

	1979	2007
CBO estimates (pretax)	0.48	0.59
CBO estimates (posttax)	0.37	0.47
Census Bureau estimates (includes transfers)	0.40	0.47
Burtless estimates (posttax, includes transfers)	0.295	0.34[a]

Sources: Krueger (2012); Burtless (2009).
Note: a. 2004 estimate.

from 0.37 to 0.47 in the same time period. Census data, which include some transfer income, report the Gini going from 0.40 in the 1970s to 0.47 in 2007. Gary Burtless, using after-tax income reported in the census in his calculations as well as accounting for public transfers, both of which reduce inequality, finds that the United States Gini grew from 0.295 in 1979 to 0.34 in 2004, an increase of 20 percent (see Burtless, 2009).[9] Based on CBO data, the market income share of the top 1 percent of households has doubled from 10 percent in the 1970s to over 20 percent in 2012, while the real household income of the bottom 10 percent grew only 3.6 percent over the same time period (Dadush et al., 2012) (see Table 2.1 for a summary of these measures).[10]

Inequality measures typically move very little or not at all for long periods of time. Thus these are remarkable trends by most countries' standards. They are almost comparable in magnitude to the remarkable increases in inequality in the former Soviet economies in the transition period, when the very equal (yet inefficient) centrally planned economies shifted to market principles, and Gini coefficients in those countries went from scores averaging 0.26 in 1990 to 0.36 in 2008 (Ortiz and Cubbins, 2011).

Inequality has increased in other countries as well—particularly the United Kingdom and Australia—and in part for the same reasons (such as dispersion between the very top of the distribution and the rest, and population

[9] One reason for the discrepancy between the two figures is that CBO has access to both Census Bureau and IRS data. Census data underreport incomes at the top, while IRS data underreport incomes at the bottom (as non-taxpayers are excluded). I thank Gary Burtless for this clarification.

[10] Not surprisingly, studies based on consumption metrics rather than incomes find smaller increases in inequality, although the time trend lines are roughly similar. See Fisher, Johnson, and Smeeding (2013).

aging). Yet trends in the United States are by far the most marked. Of all countries in the World Top Incomes Data Base, the United States has the highest shares for the top 1 percent, 0.1 percent, and 0.01 percent of earners—only South Africa and Argentina come close (Burtless, 2009; Dadush et al., 2012). Inequality trends in the United States display a U-shape curve since the booming 1920s, with inequality decreasing in the depression and post-depression years up until the 1970s, and then starting to increase again after that. While inequality in the early years was driven by differences between the owners of capital and the rest of the population, in the past decades it has primarily been due to differences in the wages of those at the top and the rest. The working rich have replaced rentiers at the top of the distribution (Piketty and Saez, 2003).

In contrast, in the past decade several countries in Latin America, a region known for some of the highest and most persistent rates of inequality in the world, have managed to make some inroads into reducing them. The Gini coefficient for the region as a whole fell from 0.54 in 2002 to 0.47 in 2014 (Gasperini, Cruces, and Tornaralli, 2016). Argentina, Brazil, and Uruguay led these trends, followed by Mexico and Peru. Much but not all of these decreases are attributed to progressive social transfer programs, such as Progresa and Oportunidades in Mexico and the Bolsa Familiar in Brazil (Lustig, Pessino, and Scott, 2013). Even then, while household surveys show decreases in inequality, the few rare studies that exist based on tax return data show a growing gap between the very top of the distribution and the rest of the population. In Chile, a new study has found that the bulk of its high levels of inequality is driven by differences between the top 1 percent —indeed the top 0.1 percent and 0.01 percent—and the rest of the distribution. In Colombia, the top 1 percent of the distribution accounts for 20 percent of total income (for Chile, see López, Figueroa, and Gutiérrez, 2013; and for Colombia, see Alvaredo and Londono Veliz, 2013).

Understanding the Causes of Inequality Trends

What explains the dramatic changes in the United States? Gary Burtless, who has provided perhaps the most encompassing explanation for these trends, focuses on four related demographic explanations, while accepting that trade and skill-driven growth also play a role. These are the aging of the population, the increase of single-parent homes, assortative mating, and migration (see Burtless, 2009).

As populations age, as they have in the United States, and the percentage past the retirement age grows larger, an increasing number of adults depend solely on pensions and public transfers for support. Since pensions and public transfers are typically lower than pre-retirement wages, the annual incomes of many families will typically be very small, pushing up inequality.

At the same time, other changes in the composition of the population have had notable effects on inequality. A growing percentage of nonelderly adults and children live in single-headed households, where they are more likely to be poor than they would be in families headed by two adults. On the other side of the spectrum, meanwhile, rising female employment rates have coincided with a higher correlation between spousal earnings, as similarly educated and skilled individuals seem more likely to marry each other (assortative mating). At the top end of the income distribution, high earning individuals are more likely to have two income earners in one household, while at the bottom end there is a higher likelihood of single-headed households, driving up inequality. A number of studies agree that changes in family living arrangements and other demographic traits account for approximately one-quarter of the upward trend in U.S. inequality.

Finally, migration also pushes up inequality, as it increases the numbers of low-skilled, low-earning workers at the bottom end of the distribution. While less than 5 percent of the resident U.S. population had been born abroad in 1970 and recent immigrants earned 17 percent less than natives, by the end of the 1990s 11 percent of the U.S. population had been born abroad and recent immigrants earned 34 percent less than natives (Burtless, 2009). While these workers typically earn markedly higher wages than they did in their home countries (and they come to the United States voluntarily), they contribute to the demographic drivers of inequality. (The effects of this, however, might be quite different in other countries where skilled immigration is the predominant trend.)

Of course there are other significant factors in addition to demographic trends. Many economists highlight the role of skill-biased technological change over the past three decades, which has driven up the wage gap between those with and without a college education (Acemoglu and Autor,

2012; Autor and Dom, 2012). Recent research by Mishel, Schmitt, and Shierholz (2013) contends that the role of skill-driven technological change was more important in the 1970s and 1980s, while other factors have played a larger role since.

One such factor is the proliferation of high salaries earned in the financial sector. In 2005 executives from finance and real estate made one-quarter of the income in the top 0.1 percent of the distribution (Krueger, 2012). Jonathan Rothwell (2016) estimates that "gratuitous pay"—i.e., pay that is above and beyond what skill differences across sectors would yield—has increased dramatically since 1980. Workers in securities and investment saw their excess pay rise from 41 percent to 60 percent between 1980 and 2013. Legal services went from 27 percent to 37 percent. Hospitals went from 21 percent to 39 percent. Meanwhile, those working in eating and drinking establishments consistently hovered around negative 20 percent. Globalization also has played a role, although it is difficult to precisely measure it. While some American workers have benefited from increased demand for the goods and services that they produce, others have been left behind as the products they produce have been crowded out by those produced more cheaply and efficiently as countries such as China have rapidly adopted cutting-edge technology.

James Galbraith (2012), based on a worldwide data set that looks at mean wages across cohorts of workers, highlights the role of financial deregulation, the IT boom, and the fiscal effects of the Bush II wars as contributors to inequality trends in the United States (as well as to the roots of the 2008–2009 financial crisis). He notes that these factors all played a role in changes in inequality being driven by a small number of people getting ahead of everyone else (often termed top-driven inequality). Similarly, Alan Krueger (2012) notes that the share of income going to the very top of the distribution has reached levels not experienced since the roaring twenties, with the share accruing to the top 1 percent of the distribution increasing by 13.5 percentage points from 1979 to 2007. This is equivalent to shifting $1.1 trillion in annual income to the top 1 percent of families. This increase in incomes for the top exceeds the total amount of income that the bottom 40 percent of households receives. These trends at the top are one reason Krueger has focused on the Gatsby curve and its implications for the next generation.

Another factor, also highlighted by Krueger (2012), is institutional. Union membership in the United States has declined from 20 percent of employees in 1983 to 12 percent today. And, perhaps not unrelated, the real value of the minimum wage fell in the 1980s. Tax policy has also contributed. While progressive, tax changes in the early 2000s benefited the very wealthy much more than other taxpayers, compounding the existing gap in pretax earnings. Tax rates for the wealthiest 0.1 percent of the population have been declining for the past five decades. And, in general, the U.S. income tax code is less progressive than those in most other OECD countries. Among OECD nations, only Chile, Korea, and Switzerland have tax codes that reduce inequality by less than that in the United States.

Mobility Rates

An obvious question is if these trends matter. If they are simply an increase in "constructive" inequality, rewarding productivity and innovation, then they should not be consequential. If they are, however, destructive, concentrating rewards and opportunities in the hands of a privileged few, while creating disincentives for investments in education and labor markets for other cohorts (in other words inequality of opportunities resulting in inequality of outcomes), then they should be of great concern. For the most part in recent years in the United States, the latter has been the case. While the United States had exceptionally high mobility rates compared to countries of comparable income levels for decades, a number of studies suggest that this is unfortunately no longer the case, in part due to trends in inequality in the past decades (Isaacs, Sawhill, and Haskins, 2008; Sawhill and Morton, 2007; Kopczuk, Saez, and Song, 2007; Congressional Budget Office, 2011). Still, the mobility story remains complex.

Krueger (2012), for example, cites recent work that finds that a worker's initial position in the income distribution is highly predictive of how much he or she earns later in his or her career. Men's income mobility has fallen since the 1970s, for example, although women's pay has increased (largely due to changes in labor force attachments over the career, with women and particularly high-skilled women more likely to be working full-time throughout their prime years. A new study by Auten, Gee, and Turner (2013), based on 1987 data from the Statistics of Income and tax return data from 2007 in the IRS Compliance Data Warehouse, finds that there is still meaningful movement across quintiles in the United States. While those in the highest quintile in 1987 have the highest probability of being in the top in 2007, there are individuals who start from the bottom or middle and move to the top and vice versa. Of those who started in the bottom quintile in 1987, 4.5 percent moved to the top quintile and some even reached the top 1 percent of the distribution. Similarly, nearly one-fourth of those in the top quintile moved down one quintile and 6.4 percent fell to the lowest quintile.[11]

Richard Reeves (2014) provides an excellent review of what we know now about the current state of social mobility in the United States in a recent Brookings Essay. A few key points are worth highlighting here. Children born on the bottom rung of the income ladder have a four in ten chance of remaining stuck there in adulthood (between 36 percent and 43 percent, depending on the data set), and a very slim chance (between 4 percent and 10 percent) of making it to the top. A child raised by a poor, unmarried mother, meanwhile, has a 50 percent risk of remaining stuck on the bottom rung, and just a 5 percent chance of making it to the top. And there are stark differences in mobility rates for different racial groups, especially between Caucasians and African Americans. Half the black children growing up on the bottom rung remain stuck there as adults (51 percent), compared to just one in four whites (23 percent).

Cross-country comparisons of intergenerational income mobility are scarce, as complete and comparable time series data for intergenerational mobility are available for only a handful of rich countries—Scandinavia, the United States, the United Kingdom, and possibly Canada. The remaining OECD countries—Germany, France, Italy, Spain, and Japan, for example—do not have good cross-generation income data covering long time periods. And the better the income data in countries like the United States, the higher the estimated correlation of parent-child income. Thus, comparisons of bad data from, for example, France, with good data from the United States could produce spurious results. Indeed, the initial sociological studies from the 1970s that highlighted exceptional rates of mobility for the United States were not based on extensive cross-country data.[12] Thus conclusions

---

[11] The authors warn about the effects of attrition, which is highest in the lowest quintile, where the probability of dying during the time period was higher.

[12] I thank Gary Burtless for raising this point. For a more recent review, see Corak (2006).

about trends in intergenerational mobility and comparisons across countries must be read with caution.

Research by Jason Long and Joseph Ferrie (2013) based on longitudinal data for the nineteenth century for the United States and Britain finds that the United States indeed had more intergenerational mobility than Britain in the nineteenth century. Yet by the second half of the twentieth century, that difference disappeared, and intergenerational mobility rates were essentially identical in the two countries. The gap was closed by decreasing mobility rates in the United States rather than increasing mobility rates in Britain. The authors explain the "exceptional" nineteenth-century period in U.S. mobility rates, to the extent they can, in part by the high levels of residential mobility in the United States compared to Britain (and greater returns to internal migration in the United States than in Britain). For the United States, the nineteenth century was the height of population growth in urban areas, while that had already occurred in Britain. Another part of the story is the growth in the advantage of white-collar workers in the United States over time (and the increasing linkages between white-collar, high-skill jobs and access to high-quality education). This has been driven by rewards to technology and skill-driven growth on the one hand, and the decreasing number and relative returns to blue-collar jobs on the other. While in the nineteenth century getting a white-collar job rather than a farm job was eleven times more likely for the son of a white-collar worker than of a farmer, by the twentieth century that advantage had grown nearly eightfold.[13]

These data, meanwhile, do not capture mobility trends among migrant workers coming to the United States from other countries (or among their children). Yet, as noted by Burtless (2009), the majority of migrants (and in particular illegal migrants) come into blue-collar rather than white-collar jobs. Thus they tend to earn lower wages than natives. An exception to this are those few privileged workers who are able to come to the United States on

[13] Some of these changes were driven by differences in levels of economic development in the United States and Britain in the nineteenth century; while the flight out of agriculture was complete by then in Britain, it was not in the United States. Thus in America in the nineteenth century, the farm sector was relatively larger, and selective exit from farming was less apparent in Britain than it was in the United States. Another possible factor in the nineteenth century United States was the existence of a public alternative to private education.

H-1B (high-skilled worker) visas,[14] although this group is not large enough to significantly alter these broader trends.

Accepting these limitations, the available data for the United States highlight a strong correlation between parents' and children's income—around 0.50. The statistic on intergenerational income mobility, the Intergenerational Income Elasticity (IGE), puts the United States at approximately 0.4. As such, if someone's parents earned 50 percent more than the average, their child can be expected to earn 20 percent above the average for their generation. And parental income matters more in the United States than in the other countries for which we have data, challenging the traditional image of the United States as the land of opportunity. The IGE, meanwhile, is higher when income inequality is higher. In the United States, it is predicted to increase from 0.47 to 0.56 as a result of recent inequality trends (Krueger, 2012).

The Economic Mobility Project, undertaken by the Pew Charitable Trust and the Brookings Institution, estimates that 40 percent of children born to parents in the bottom quintile of the distribution will remain there, and 60 percent will move up, but not likely far above the bottom quintile. In contrast, a child born into a family in the top 5 percent of the income distribution has a 22 percent chance of remaining in the top as an adult. There are also large racial differences. White workers are ten times more likely than are African American workers to make it into the top 25 percent of the income distribution. One of the most important linkages to upward mobility in the United States, meanwhile, is access to a high-quality education, which is, in turn, highly correlated with parental incomes (Isaacs, Sawhill, and Haskins, 2008; Dadush et al., 2012).

Auten, Gee, and Turner (2013) discover modestly higher rates of mobility for a shorter and more defined period of time: 1987 to 2007. They find that 30 percent of dependents from families in the lowest quintile in 1987 were themselves in the lowest quintile relative to those of the same age in 2007. Approximately one-fifth rose to each of the next three quintiles, 11 percent rose to the top quintile, and some made it to the top 1 percent. Meanwhile, 41 percent of those from families in the top quintile were themselves in the top quintile in 2007 (again, relative to those of the same age in 2007), while

---

[14]For detail on H-1B workers, see Ruiz and Wilson (2013).

25 percent, 16 percent, and 9 percent moved down one, two, or three quintiles, respectively.

One attempt to construct international mobility comparisons is the World Bank's Index of Economic Opportunity (IEO), led by Francisco Ferreira (Ferreira, 2013; Brunori, Ferreira, and Peragine, 2013). Roemer's birth lottery provides a conceptual basis. The index attempts to deepen our understanding of intergenerational mobility trends by unbundling inequality into two distinct components: that which people can control and is the result of differential skills and efforts, and that which is associated with circumstances that people do not control, such as their race, gender, place of birth, or family background. Populations are divided into various subgroups, each of which is homogenous in terms of predetermined circumstances (called "types"). In a world of equal opportunities, there would be no difference between income distributions characterizing each of these subgroups.

The IEO indicates the share of overall inequality that is accounted for by inequality between the mean incomes of those subgroups (types). It has been computed for a number of countries, with the most equal being Norway (2 percent) and the least equal being Guatemala (34 percent). The United States falls somewhere in the middle of the distribution, above Spain, India, Great Britain, Brazil, and Peru, but well below Norway, Poland, Hungary, and Italy, to name a few.

As noted in the introduction and discussed in later chapters, the distribution of well-being in the United States has also grown more unequal (Helliwell, Layard, and Sachs, 2013; Clark, Fleche, and Senik, 2016). The trends in the United States are likely due to an increase in unhappiness among the poor and vulnerable rather than greater happiness among already happy (on average) wealthy cohorts. The potential implications of these and related trends in well-being for the future of these different cohorts are the focus of the rest of the book.

Despite the evidence showing increasing inequality of income, opportunity, and even well-being in the United States for many years, public perceptions of inequality have not changed commensurately. There have been some signs of change in recent years (discussed in Chapter 3). The persistence in these beliefs is at least in part due to the fact that historically there has been a strong conviction that the value of individual effort is what matters. Indeed, beginning with de Tocqueville, America was seen as the land of opportunity, and there are still millions of immigrants who come to the United States seeking and finding opportunities that they do not have at home. It may also be reinforced by the high visibility of successful—and often generous— individuals who remain iconoclasts in U.S. society, such as Bill Gates, Warren Buffett, and Michael Bloomberg, among others. Finally, as is noted above, there is likely a lag in public attitudes, and very visible markers of change are more effective at generating shifts in attitudes than gradual trends.

Inequality is still, at least for some Americans to some extent, a signal of successful individual effort. Yet for most of those concentrated in the bottom of the distribution, it is becoming a disincentive to making investments in a future that is increasingly determined by the birth lottery.

No Longer a Land of Equal Opportunity?

This chapter has highlighted how complex it is to measure inequality, both because of its many different facets, each of which can matter differently to different people, and because of the complexity of the metrics that are used and the different conclusions that can be drawn from the manner in which the metrics are deployed. Measuring trends in opportunity and mobility is made even more difficult because the over-time data that are necessary to do so are scarce. Well-being metrics give us an insight into the effects of inequality on individual welfare, meanwhile, but also highlight the many ways in which inequality and well-being interact and affect individual attitudes and behaviors.

Despite these complexities, it is clear from every metric available that inequality has increased dramatically in the United States—relative both to the past and to most other countries. And while the linkages with trends in opportunity and income mobility are less clear, there is sufficient evidence to suggest that they are important in a number of ways. The available evidence suggests that we are not the Horatio Alger society the United States has long been reputed to be and that there are very large differences in the opportunities and life choices that different socioeconomic and racial cohorts in this country have.

Perhaps the starkest trend is that well-being—as measured by life satisfaction, aspirations for the future, and a range of other markers—has also become more unequal in the United States in recent years. Significant sectors of U.S. society are not able to achieve the American Dream of "the pursuit of happiness" in its fullest sense. The implications of these trends and of the unequally shared dream, and for disadvantaged socioeconomic cohorts in particular, are the subject of the rest of the book.

CHAPTER 3

Who Believes in the American Dream?

Public Attitudes about Mobility in the United States and Beyond

I'm a great believer in luck, and the harder I work, the more I have of it.[1]

This insight—that we often create opportunities through our own agency—highlights an important relationship between beliefs and behavior. Optimistic people are more likely to invest in their own futures, not least because they believe in them (Graham, Eggers, and Sukhtankar, 2004; De Neve and Oswald, 2012; De Neve et al., 2013). Optimism and belief in agency typically coincide, as in part they reflect realistic assessments. Wealthier and more educated people are more likely to assess their futures positively, and have good grounds for doing so. But accurate forecasting of life chances is not the whole story. Positive beliefs can also have an independent impact on outcomes, and may be particularly important for those with fewer means.

Strong faith in the role of individual effort in getting people ahead is part and parcel of the American Dream. The image of America as the land of opportunity has long been a source of national pride as well as an explanation for the dynamism of the American economy. It is also one of the central explanations for poor Americans' tolerance for high levels of inequality and the more

---

[1] This quote is often attributed to Thomas Jefferson, but there is some controversy over whether it was really said by him, with the Jefferson library noting that it is a spurious attribution. Other possible sources are Mark Twain, George Allen, Samuel Goldwyn, and an "old Amish saying." I thank Jon Rauch for noting that. Regardless of the source, the relevance of the quote to the chapter holds.

general lack of political support for redistribution. In well-known theoretical work, Bénabou and Ok (2001) posit that because of this long-held perception of inequality as a sign of future mobility, the majority of voters believe they will be above mean income in the future (even though that is a mathematical impossibility) and do not want to vote to tax themselves or their children.[2]

There is still good reason to have faith in the individual work ethic and its ability to get people ahead in the United States. Indeed, millions of migrants continue to come to America to escape dire poverty, and not only stay but end up providing much better lives for their children. Yet there is also increasing evidence, discussed in Chapter 2, of the barriers to rising to the top for cohorts who start at the bottom, and of the persistently greater advantages that those at the top have to remaining there. The disadvantages of being born into particular races and/or family structures, meanwhile, are both more evident and more persistent at the bottom of the distribution.

Not surprisingly, beliefs in the American Dream are no longer as widely shared as they used to be. Nor are Americans' beliefs in individual effort and hard work exceptional compared to other countries and regions. Does this matter?

The Relationship between Inequality and Well-Being

There is no conclusive evidence about the relationship between inequality and well-being, with some studies finding a positive relationship and others a negative one. My own work suggests that this is because inequality signals different things in different contexts. In some it serves as a sign of potential future progress—as it was in the United States, at least until recently. In others it is a sign of persistent advantage for some cohorts and persistent disadvantage for others.

There are also lags in public perceptions, and inequality signals do not always reflect the most recent trends in particular contexts. Tolerance for inequality persisted in the United States for decades as it was increasing

---

[2]Peyton Young and I (Graham and Young, 2003) took a cursory look at attitudes about redistribution and inequality at the time of the Bush tax cuts (2002–2003) and were surprised to see that polls showed that while only one half of the top 1 percent of Americans in the income distribution actually benefited from the tax cuts, 19 percent of Americans thought they would when they were proposed, and therefore did not pose political opposition to them.

markedly, for example. In contrast, public frustration with inequality in many countries in Latin America remained high while absolute mobility was on the rise and inequality was gradually falling. As the data I present later in the chapter show, attitudes in Latin America have changed, but long after actual trends in the distribution.

Another reason for these mixed results is the distinction between comparative and normative reference groups (Clark and D'Ambrosio, 2015). A comparative reference group acts as the standard of comparison for self-appraisal. A normative reference group is the source of norms, attitudes, and values of the individuals concerned. Both groups can be further distinguished by whether the individual in question is or is not a member of the reference group. Comparative reference groups suggest that one's own position relative to others matters, even if the individual is not in the group but aspires to be. In contrast, in the normative view of reference groups, inequality is evaluated by individuals regardless of where they are in the distribution or even in it at all.

The authors note that "the normative evaluation of an income distribution can also be thought of as a mirror of preferences over inequality under the veil of ignorance" (Clark and D'Ambrosio, 2015, p. 1151). This quote refers to philosopher John Rawls's veil of ignorance, in which he posits that when people choose the level of redistribution that they think is optimal for society, they should do so from a position in which they do not know where they start out—in other words, they should be completely ignorant about whether they are advantaged or disadvantaged at birth.

Because of the available measures, most of the debate, at least among economists, has been about measured trends in income inequality and sometimes, although less often, about over-time trends in mobility. Yet regardless of trends in the data, the channel by which inequality likely has the most direct effects on individual welfare and resulting behaviors is what it signals in different societies and among different cohorts. These signals are part and parcel of the channel between beliefs and behavioral outcomes. Signals also differ depending on the particular reference group for inequality (for example, the firm level, neighborhood level, city level, country level, and so on).

Studies of inequality and individual well-being—in the United States, the European Union, and Latin America—get mixed results. Some find a negative correlation between inequality and life satisfaction, others find weak results, and some even find a positive correlation (Alesina, Di Tella, and MacCulloch, 2004; Graham and Felton, 2006; Oishi, Kesebir, and Diener, 2011; Van Praag and Ferrer-i-Carbonell, 2009). Alesina, Di Tella, and MacCulloch (2004) compare the well-being effects of inequality on Americans (across states) and Europeans (across countries). They find that inequality has a modest negative effect on the well-being of Europeans, particularly poor ones. The only group in their comparison that incurs well-being losses from inequality in the United States, however, is left-leaning rich people!

Erzo Luttmer (2005) uses a different reference group, closer to the neighborhood level (Public Use Microdata Areas or PUMAs), finds a negative correlation between average neighborhood-level incomes and life satisfaction in the United States, and highlights the negative role of comparison effects (which may be more salient at the local level than at the statewide level). In contrast, in Russia Claudia Senik (2009) finds a positive effect of average regional-level incomes, suggesting a role for positive signaling effects in contexts of uncertainty and transition.

Richard Burkhauser, Jan-Emmanuel De Neve, and Nick Powdthavee (2015) look at the effects of top incomes—such as the share of income held by the top 1 percent in countries around the world, based on Gallup World Poll and tax data from the World Top Income Database. Due to the availability of the latter, their sample is primarily composed of developed economies, with the exception of South Africa. They find that a higher share of income held by the top 1 percent is associated with lower levels of evaluative well-being (life satisfaction) and higher levels of negative emotion (stress, anger, worry, and pain), controlling for per capita GDP, own incomes, and a range of other socioeconomic and demographic traits.

They also use the British Household Panel to look at trends within one country over time, and get similar findings. They explain their findings with a "status anxiety" model, among other possible explanations, as the more income is top concentrated, the less attainable that status seems to be for the average person. The negative effects are stronger for more educated than less educated cohorts, supporting such an explanation, as more educated cohorts are more likely to be aware of what top levels are, and also more likely to have aspirations of reaching them.

In new work in progress, John Ifcher, Homa Zarghamee, and I (2017) explore the well-being effect of relative incomes at the zip code and MSA (metropolitan statistical area)[3] levels in the United States, based on Gallup Daily Poll data. We find that individual incomes have the expected positive effect on life satisfaction. Yet higher median levels of MSA-level incomes have a negative effect on life satisfaction and are also positively correlated with stress and other markers of ill-being. Interestingly and by way of contrast, we find that higher levels of median zip-code-level income have a modest but positive effect. We posit that cost of living and comparative effects may dominate more in larger scale reference areas, such as cities or states, while positive externalities associated with higher income levels, such as better local amenities and public goods, seem to dominate in smaller reference areas, such as neighborhoods.

Angus Deaton and Arthur Stone (2013) use Gallup Healthways data for the United States and examine the relationship between both evaluative and hedonic dimensions of well-being and inequality at the zip code level. As do Ifcher, Zarghamee, and I, they find that both individual-level income and average zip-code-level income are positively correlated with evaluative well-being. Both sets of findings suggest a positive effect of living in a place where average income levels are higher. This makes sense if living with wealthier people provides better public goods and other externalities that enhance well-being over the long term. In contrast, Deaton and Stone find that hedonic well-being, as measured by happiness yesterday, is either negatively correlated or insignificant with average zip-code-level incomes, and the coefficient on individual-level income is an order of magnitude smaller. Thus hedonic well-being is less affected by income in general, but possibly more negatively affected by higher income differentials, such as one's neighbor having a much bigger house or better car.

Evaluative and hedonic well-being questions capture different aspects of human well-being, which in turn relate differently to income and to income differentials. The best possible life question, which asks respondents to compare their lives to the best possible life they can imagine and is the evaluative well-being question in Gallup polls, introduces a relative component. As such, it heightens the importance of income (and related status) for respondents. Questions that ask "Were you happy yesterday?" or "Did you smile frequently yesterday?" are much more open and capture a range of unobserved

[3] MSAs are larger areas than zip codes but smaller than U.S. states.

experiences and values that could influence responses. In more technical terms, happy yesterday likely picks up more unobserved "noise" in the data (and people's lives and experiences) that may or may not be related to income.[4]

In Latin America, poverty and inequality rates have decreased in recent years, and (to the extent we have data) there are signs that mobility rates have increased (Lopez-Calva and Lustig, 2010). Yet, as noted above, public perceptions have been slow to catch up. Andrew Felton and I (Graham and Felton, 2006) looked at the relationship between inequality and happiness in Latin America in 2006, based on a large, region-wide data set, the Latinobarómetro.[5]

In contrast to the mixed findings for the United States, we found that inequality (defined as each respondent's distance from average income for his or her country, controlling for average per capita income in each country) had strong negative effects for the happiness of the poor and positive effects for the happiness of the rich. Average per capita income had no significant effect on happiness, meanwhile. Thus, at least until recently in Latin America, relative income differences had far more important effects on reported happiness than did absolute income levels. Our more recent analysis—based on data that span the period 2005 to 2013 and are presented below—suggests that this may be changing, albeit with a long lag.

We also looked at respondents in cities of different sizes (small—fewer than 5,000 inhabitants, medium—from 10,000 to 100,000 inhabitants, and large—over 100,000 respondents) to see if our results varied when we used different reference groups. We found that the negative effects of inequality were greater in larger cities, as one would expect, as both wealth differences

[4] For more detail on these questions, see Graham, Chattopadhyay, and Picon (2010b).

[5] The Latinobarómetro (1997–2008) survey consists of approximately one thousand annual interviews in each of eighteen countries in Latin America. The samples are conducted by a prestigious research firm in each country, and are nationally representative except for Chile, Colombia, and Paraguay. The survey is comparable to the Eurobarometer survey for European countries in design and focus; both surveys are cross sections rather than panels. A standard set of demographic questions is asked every year. The usual problems with accurately measuring income in developing countries where most respondents work in the informal sector and cannot record a fixed salary are present. Many surveys rely on reported expenditures, which tend to be more accurate, if less good at capturing the assets of the very wealthy. The Latinobarómetro has neither, and instead relies on the interviewer's assessment of household socioeconomic status (SES) as well as a long list of questions about ownership of goods and assets, upon which we compile our wealth index. The index is based on ownership of eleven types of assets, ranging from drinking water and plumbing to computers and second homes.

and aspirations are greater. In addition, we found that the only context where average incomes were positively related to well-being was small cities. One can imagine that in smaller places, where people are more connected with one another and poverty is still a widespread concern, higher levels of average incomes may have positive signaling and spillover effects that counter the usual comparison effects, as in the case of our zip code findings for the United States. The effects of relative income differences were still negative for those below mean income in the small cities in Latin America, however.

One reason for the misalignment between perceptions and actual trends in many contexts is the complex nature of most income inequality data, which makes it quite difficult for the average citizen to discern. It is hard to imagine that average people on the street will find a meaningful difference between a Gini coefficient of 0.43 and 0.47, for example. They are much more likely to notice if the neighbors build a bigger house, as they might have in the precrisis boom, and/or if they lose their big house to foreclosure, as they might have in the postcrisis period.

A recent study carried out in the United States by Nishi et al. (2015), based on experiments in social networks, finds that inequality seems to matter only when it is visible. As such, when respondents had more information about their neighbor's or network member's wealth, they became less trusting and less cooperative and less likely to support redistribution to fund neighborhood-level public goods. The visibility finding again highlights the importance of the reference group that is used and/or available. Inequality seems to matter more if it is at a level that it can be both perceived and understood (such as visible displays of wealth at the neighborhood level) and within a reference group that individuals can relate to, such as social networks or small towns, rather than at the broader national or global levels.

Another recent study by Perez-Truglia (2016) takes advantage of a 2001 regulatory change in Norway, which mandated that all income tax records be publicly accessible online, and explores the effects on well-being. He finds that that increased transparency in tax data—and therefore individuals' knowledge about their rank in the income distribution—increased the gradient of the happiness-income relationship, thereby making those higher up in the rankings relatively happier. At the same time, it increased the happiness gap between the rich and the poor by 29 percent. The increased knowledge about individual rank may have reduced the well-being of those at the bottom by making them more aware of how much less they had than those at the top.

These findings resonate with recent research by Clark and Senik (2015) in China. They find that average village income is positively correlated with financial satisfaction, but being in a low rank in the distribution in the same village is negatively correlated. Knight and Gunatilaka (2014) find that rural respondents in China typically compare their financial situation to that of their own household in the past year, while urban respondents compare their situation with the average for their city or large village. Recent migrants to urban areas are most bothered by inequality, likely because they have just become aware of how much lower their incomes are compared to the average in their new cities (Kingdon and Knight, 2007).

Some new work by Alexandru Cojocaru (forthcoming), based on a comparison of Western and Eastern Europe and using the Life in Transition survey—a large survey of transition economies that started in the mid-1990s and runs through the present—tests the signaling hypothesis explicitly. He compares respondents based on their past mobility trends and on their attitudes about the fairness of the distribution. He finds that respondents with a recent trajectory of upward mobility are less likely to support redistribution (perhaps because they feel that they worked very hard to get ahead), as are those who believe that success is a result of hard work (as opposed to luck and connections).

Cojocaru also tests the mediating effects of different reference norms. He finds that with a reference norm that is imposed by the researcher, in this case distance from the Census Enumeration Area mean income, inequality in that area has inconsistent effects on reported well-being. In contrast, with a self-assessed reference group—the respondents' reported position on a notional societal economic ladder—inequality has a strong and significant correlation with well-being. The economic ladder question asks respondents to rank their position in society compared to the rich (at the top of the ladder) and the poor (at the bottom).[6] In the transition context, what inequality

---

[6] The variable is actually the respondent's score in the last year of the survey minus the respondent's score in the first year of the survey. As with any study based on perceptions and well-being, there is an endogeneity problem, as less happy respondents may be more likely to perceive injustice or to compare themselves negatively with others. As a robustness check, Cojocaru uses an instrumental variables strategy, based on the interviewer's assessments of each household's rank in their community, and his findings still hold.

signals clearly mediates its effects on well-being, and how much it matters varies depending on whether the reference group is arbitrarily imposed or chosen by the respondent. (Of course, individuals who are less satisfied with their lives and/or more concerned about inequality may place themselves lower on ladder.)

Cojocaru's findings are analogous, in a way, to the trends across Democrats and Republicans in the United States. Democrats have traditionally perceived outcomes to be a result of systemic bias rather than personal effort, and are more likely to be concerned about injustice, while Republicans are more likely to believe that outcomes are a result of personal effort in the labor market. Not surprisingly, Democrats are both less happy about inequality and less happy in general than are Republicans (Graham, Chattopadhyay, and Picon 2010a).

Finally, a very new study by Johannes Haushofer, James Reisinger, and Jeremy Shapiro (2015) looks at the well-being effects of cash transfers in villages in Kenya. Taking advantage of a randomized control trial, where some villagers received transfers and others did not, they find that that an increase of $100 in mean village wealth causes a 0.11 standard deviation decrease in life satisfaction among individuals in the households that did not receive transfers; in other words, while average wealth and average life satisfaction went up, the households that did not receive transfers experienced a sharp decrease from the average. The (negative) magnitude of that change is more than four times that of a (positive) change in own wealth by the same amount. As such, comparison effects also hold in extremely poor contexts. And, because the income received was in the form of transfers and luck, rather than earned income, comparison effects are probably more relevant than signaling effects to those who did not receive the transfers.

Inequality thus has varied effects on well-being, and they are mediated by what inequality signals, as well as the reference group that is utilized. In smaller (and likely poorer) reference groups, the positive effects of higher levels of average income seem to outweigh the negative comparison effects from relative income differences, even though concerns about rank still hold. In larger reference groups, such as big cities, where social connections are weaker (and resources are less likely to be pooled) and where income variance is much greater, comparison effects often overwhelm the effects of higher average income levels, and concerns about rank may even be more important.

What inequality signals—or more importantly what people believe it signals—is a critical part of the relationship between beliefs and behaviors. If the signals are positive, then people are more likely to see inequality as an incentive or as a just reward for hard work. If the signals are negative and inequality is perceived as a sign of injustice or of persistent disadvantage for some groups and advantage for others (including in ability), it can serve as a disincentive to hard work and to investing in the future.

Inequality and Mobility Beliefs: What Do We Know?

In Chapter 2, I discussed Richard Reeves's (2014) review of a large body of work documenting the current state of social mobility in the United States. The strong linkages that Reeves highlights between parents' and children's outcomes, as well as large differences across races, are not the reality that has driven exceptional American attitudes about future mobility for many decades. We know less about the extent to which public perceptions grasp this reality and how attitudes have changed. It is likely that they have, not least given the widespread public attention to the issue of inequality in the 2016 electoral debate.

As noted above, for decades U.S. citizens accepted and even supported exceptionally high rates of inequality and low rates of redistributive taxation because of this widely held belief in the inequality-opportunity link. While we know that outcomes in the United States are diverging and that attitudes are also starting to change, we know much less about the behavioral dimensions (including well-being) underlying them, and how they vary across cohorts.

A recent Pew survey on American attitudes about mobility and inequality (cited in Reeves, 2014) provides some evidence that American attitudes are no longer exceptional. In all, 61 percent of Americans think the economic system favors the wealthy, while only 35 percent think it is fair to most people. This compares (negatively) to 44 percent of Australians reporting that the system favors the wealthy and 51 percent saying it is fair to most, and is about on par with the 65 percent of respondents in Great Britain (which is hardly known for exceptional rates of mobility) saying it favors the wealthy and 30 percent saying that it is fair to most.

Perhaps most significant of all, at least in terms of faith in future mobility, a remarkably high 62 percent of Americans think that their children will be worse off than they are, and only 33 percent think they will do better. While this is not a particularly hopeful picture, Americans are, for the most part, more optimistic than most of their counterparts in the OECD, with some exceptions, such as Australia (where only 53 percent think their children will be worse off, and 37 percent better). Yet respondents in the emerging market countries and in LAC in particular are much more hopeful. Only 13 percent of Chileans and 38 percent of Argentines think that their children will be worse off than they are. And while Americans still demonstrate faith in hard work (more so than residents in many countries), that has fallen in recent decades. Of those surveyed in the Pew poll, 60 percent responded that "most people who want to get ahead can make it if they are willing to work hard," but that is down from 68 percent in 1994 (Reeves, 2014).

Judith Niehaus at the Cologne-based IW Institute found that as late as 2014, most Europeans (in a sample of twenty-three countries) thought that their societies are far less equal than they are, while most Americans believed that their society is more equal than it is. Europeans underestimated the proportion of middle-income earners and overestimated the proportion of poor (defined as those with 60 percent or less than median income); the United States had the opposite trend (Niehaus, 2014, cited in Wagstyl, 2014).

Yet, as noted above, U.S. attitudes on inequality are also divided across ideological lines, even more so than in other countries with more equal distributions of income. A recent Pew poll found that 57 percent of Republicans believed that people who became rich did so because they worked harder than others, while only 27 percent of Democrats did. In contrast, only 32 percent of Republicans felt that people were poor because of circumstances beyond their control, compared to 63 percent of Democrats (Blow, 2014). There is less available evidence of how these attitudes vary across socioeconomic and racial cohorts; this is something that our new data analysis, discussed below, attempts to shed light on.

There is also more evidence that concerns about inequality have increased across the board. A 2015 poll asked this question: "Which comes closer to your view? In today's economy, everyone has a fair chance to get ahead in the long run, or in today's economy, it's mainly just a few people at the top who have a chance to get ahead." Only 35 percent of respondents answered that anyone can get ahead, while 61 percent thought that just a few people at the top had that chance. And 67 percent of respondents thought that the gap between the rich and poor was getting larger, while only 5 percent thought it was getting smaller (Scheiber and Sussman, 2015).

These concerns are also demonstrated by shrinking faith in the American Dream. In response to a June 2015 poll of two thousand respondents conducted by the Atlantic and the Aspen Institute, 75 percent said that the American Dream was "suffering," while just one-quarter said that it was alive and well. Rather remarkably, whites were the most pessimistic racial group, compared to blacks and Hispanics (Berman, 2015). This also corroborates with our findings, discussed in Chapter 4, on differences in future outlooks across racial and socioeconomic cohorts in the United States, where we find poor whites to be the most pessimistic about the future.

There may also be some gradual changes in ideological affiliation, meanwhile. A 2012 Pew Center poll reported that while low income earners in the United States are more likely to consider themselves Democrats (34 percent) than Republicans (16 percent), the percentage of high earners who affiliate with either party is the same (31 percent)—a declining trend for Republicans in the past decade. The percentage of respondents who report to be independents has increased in the same time period (reaching 38 percent in 2012) (Pew Center for People and the Press, 2012). While we cannot attribute these trends to inequality, they are, nevertheless, suggestive of some signs of shifts in support for these polarized perspectives.

Differences across Socioeconomic Cohorts

The political differences in attitudes are of interest, and surely affect voting behavior. Yet differences across socioeconomic and demographic cohorts are more relevant to public policy (or at least more likely to be influenced by it) and more likely to have longer term implications. And, as the rest of the book highlights, inequalities in income and expectations across rich and poor, different races, and/or other identifiable cohorts can result in persistent beliefs and behavior linkages. As such, it is the focus of the rest of the discussion and empirical analysis.

The nascent literature on time preferences, discount rates, and differential ability to save for and invest in the future, which is reviewed in detail in the next chapters, suggests that respondents who suffer from high levels of stress associated with daily struggles and related inability to plan ahead have much higher discount rates. In other words, they disproportionately value today's income more than tomorrow's and fail to make important investments to ensure their future, such as in health insurance or education (see, for example, Barofsky, 2015).

One view comes from a recent study of working hours. Lambert, Fugiel, and Henly (2014) find that 41 percent of hourly workers in the United States learn their schedules less than a week in advance—more than the percentage who know at least a month in advance—and half of hourly workers have no control over their schedules (perhaps because of fluctuations in demand for services in their industries). Related studies show that unpredictable working hours exacerbate stress, harm health, and attenuate work-life conflicts (Reeves, 2014).

In Latin America, meanwhile, we find that when queried about well-being, the rich are more likely to highlight the role of work and good health in their lives, while poor people are more likely to highlight friends and religion as social insurance mechanisms. Work and health allow those with means to make choices and pursue the kinds of lives they want to lead. Those without means often face a stressful and difficult daily existence, resulting in shortsighted and risk-averse decision making (Graham and Nikolova, 2015; Graham and Lora, 2009; see also Haushofer and Fehr, 2014). High levels of inequality, meanwhile, can make better future outlooks seem unattainable for poor cohorts at the bottom of the distribution, for any number of reasons.

These beliefs can be self-perpetuating. Jeff Butler's (2014) experimental work (briefly referenced in Chapter 1) shows that regardless of effort, respondents who are consistently in the low-pay experimental group believe that they have less ability, while those in the high pay group believe they have more ability, even though their actual ability/performance in the experiment tasks are no different. Our new data on hard work beliefs for the United States (discussed below), meanwhile, are also suggestive of this self-perpetuation channel, whereby those who are higher up in the income distribution are more likely to believe that hard work got them there (and perhaps also more likely to demand more pay).

A study on inequality and job satisfaction, based on panel data from Australia, also highlights this beliefs channel. The effects of inequality in pay seem to be asymmetric. While the richer individuals who earn incomes above those of their reference group have some gains in job satisfaction, the losses in job satisfaction for those who earn below their reference group incomes are much greater (Kifle, 2013). It is plausible that those earning incomes below those of their reference group perceive unfairness in compensation, while those earning above attribute their success to their own efforts (reminiscent of the Butler findings on ability beliefs).

As already noted in Chapter 1, high-ability disadvantaged students tend to choose less expensive, less prestigious schools even when offered a free education (Hoxby and Avery, 2012). The explanation is not financial but rather informational and aspirational: disadvantaged students may simply not know about the existence of grants to attend these schools, or simply may not believe they can excel in them. If elite colleges are perceived as having brighter students and completing college requires ability-based competition, disadvantage itself may diminish prospective students' assessments of the value of attending if they believe that they cannot compete.

Social psychologist Daphna Oyserman and colleagues have researched how students' identity affects how they perceive "impossible" versus "important" tasks and how they feel they rank on those tasks. Once prompted, their identity affects how much time they put into schoolwork and their performance on tasks such as Raven's test. The differences in performance were not there prior to the identity manipulation (Smith and Oyserman, 2015). Oyserman also finds that school-focused aspirations and expectations predict action by students if they are relevant. Relevance runs along three lines: social identities (race/ethnicity, social class); feeling connected with relevant behavioral strategies (studying/asking questions); and providing an interpretation of difficulties along the way as implying task importance, not impossibility (Oyserman, 2013). Without such relevance, low-income and minority children have difficulty envisioning where they will end up and the role of school in that equation.

Looking across studies, Oyserman also finds that expectations and aspirations (even among low-income kids) are always higher than actual college graduation rates. Many of them try but fail because they believe they do not fit in school. In addition to income and education, an important factor seems to be the family having a savings account and particularly one marked for college. The latter is a tangible factor signaling expectations about the future and perhaps also the feasibility of meeting those expectations.

George Akerlof—in earlier work (1997) and more recently with Rachel Kranton (2010)—highlights the role of identity interacting with expectations in determining individuals' behavior and their success in completing educational goals. Akerlof cites a famous experiment in which a New York entrepreneur, Eugene Lang, offered to give a college scholarship to every student of a fifth-grade class in Harlem. The vast majority of them were considered likely to go to college six years later, and all of those eligible were academically strong enough to obtain either loans or scholarships in absence of the Lang offer. One explanation (among others) for the success of the program was that the group nature of the offer reinforced a shared identity linked to academic success, while dropping out of high school resulted in being isolated from the peer group.

Recent work by Melissa Kearney and Phil Levine (2015) highlights the linkages between inequality, aspirations, and high school dropout rates. They investigate whether high income inequality and low social mobility lead young people from lower socioeconomic status (SES) households to drop out of high school—a decision that has important consequences for their ability to climb the economic ladder. It is already clear that income inequality and dropout rates across states and cities are correlated; the purpose of their investigation is to assess whether this correlation reflects a causal relationship.

Boys with less educated mothers are more likely to drop out of high school if they live in a state with more inequality in the bottom half of the distribution (i.e., the gap between household incomes at the 10th to 50th percentiles). This pattern does not hold for boys from higher educated families. This finding holds up in more sophisticated econometric analyses, after controlling for a host of individual and state-level characteristics. In particular, they find that moving from a low-inequality state to a high-inequality one increases the likelihood that a low-SES male student will drop out of high school by 4.1 percentage points.

Their findings hold when controlling for a range of other factors, including the industrial composition of the labor market, the demographic characteristics of the state population (including racial composition and fraction of single-parent households), rates of residential segregation by race or income, and public school financing, among other possibilities. They also examine the role of ability. Including a measure of cognitive ability at age seventeen reduces the estimate of the impact of inequality on high school dropout rates—but only slightly.

They describe their findings in the frame of an "economic despair" model (which is reminiscent of the stress/status findings of De Neve et al., 2013, outlined above). As the gap between the bottom and middle of the income distribution widens, middle-class life and economic success feel increasingly out of reach to kids from economically disadvantaged households—reminiscent of both the Hoxby and Oyserman work. They therefore lose the motivation to stay in school and try to make that climb.

As noted in Chapter 1, the differences in both real and perceived ability can begin very early on in the life cycle. Psychologists Betty Hart and Todd Risley (1995) studied the word acquisition of toddlers in the United States in the 1990s and found that there were "intractable differences in rates of vocabulary growth" depending on SES. The toddlers ranged from children of professors to those of welfare mothers (as well as many SES categories in between); the authors found that by age three, the children of professors were acquiring words at rates several times higher than the slowest learners. Meanwhile, the rates of discouragement on children's utterances (e.g., silencing or negative responses) were highest for welfare parents and lowest for professors. Their work, in turn, was predictive of findings of school research, in which children from poor families in high school lacked the vocabulary used in more advanced textbooks.

A more recent study based on the Add Health panel for the United States by Michael Shanahan and colleagues (2014) explores the linkages between personality traits and social class. They find that personality traits such as agreeableness, extraversion, imagination, and conscientiousness in the teenage years all have significant relationships with educational attainment, hourly wages, and self-direction at work later in life, effects that hold above and beyond the important role of parental education. They find that personality traits have a stronger link with outcomes at lower levels of SES, but that children from lower SES status are less likely to possess these traits. This is not genetically determined but rather because higher SES parents are more likely to encourage these traits in their children and/or because the opportunity structures facing high SES children are more likely to foster traits such as agreeableness, trust, and efficacy. Yet having these traits was more important to the attainment of low SES children because they helped substitute for low investments in human capital.

In sum, there is a difficult-to-measure but detectable relationship between inequality and beliefs, hopes, and aspirations, with higher levels of inequality (in income and nonincome dimensions) often making it more difficult for those at the bottom of the distribution to have aspirations for the future. The same evidence also shows that these differential beliefs about the future are persistent and have effects on long-term outcomes.

The American Dream from the Perspective of Well-Being Metrics

In the following section I explore the relationship between attitudes toward mobility and a range of socioeconomic and demographic traits, and in particular how these attitudes differ across the poor and the rich in the United States. I then compare patterns in the United States with those in a few other regions of the world.

Methods and Data

I use data from the Gallup World Poll and the Gallup Healthways surveys. The Gallup World Poll has been conducted annually in roughly 160 countries worldwide since 2005, with one wave per year. It has nationally representative coverage in most countries. Gallup weights the data in each country—and the sample size ranges from more than four thousand household interviews in China every year to five hundred households in Puerto Rico. While the poll covers most existing countries around the world, with very few exceptions, a drawback is that there are proportionately more responses for small countries than for large ones. Different individuals are interviewed each year, and thus we have pooled cross-sections of data—including year dummies—rather than a panel.

Gallup Healthways provided extensive data at the daily household level from January 2008 to 2013 (the last year for which we have updated data). It is a stratified sample of an average of one thousand households across the

United States (all localities with landline phones and mobile cell phone connections), surveyed almost every day for the entire period, and thus has a very large number of individual observations. The questions include the usual demographic details of the respondents (age, race, ethnicity, household size, education level), economic conditions (employment status, job security, job mobility), respondents' perceptions about their standards of living and the state of the economy, access to services (such as health insurance, medical care, telephone and Internet), geographic location (zip code, MSA, and Federal Information Processing Standards [FIPS] code), personal health, emotional experiences, and emotional conditions, among others. It is, again, cross-sectional rather than panel.[7]

As a simple first step, I compared the well-being scores of the poorest and richest Americans based on the Gallup Daily Poll. We looked at both dimensions of well-being. For the evaluative dimension I used the standard question in the Gallup Poll, the Cantril ladder question. This question asks respondents to compare their lives to the best possible life they can imagine on a ladder where 0 represents the worst life and 10 represents the best possible life (BPL).

I also used a negative hedonic question (stress), which simply asks respondents whether or not they experienced stress the day before, with possible answers being yes or no. As noted above, high levels of stress that are associated with circumstances beyond individuals' control tend to be associated with short-term time horizons and lack of ability to plan for the future, among other markers of ill-being.

Respondents in the poorest income quintile in the United States experience significantly higher levels of stress in their daily lives than do those in the highest one. They also score much lower than those in higher ones when they are asked to assess their satisfaction with their lives as a whole. The latter is a metric that captures respondents' ability to make choices and control their lives, among other things (see Figure 3.1). As a result, individuals who are living day to day and with low expectations for the future typically score much lower on evaluative questions than do those with more means and choices.

---

[7] For full disclosure, I am an academic advisor to the Gallup Polls and in that capacity have access to the data. Some tables and figures in the following section were originally published in Graham (2016).

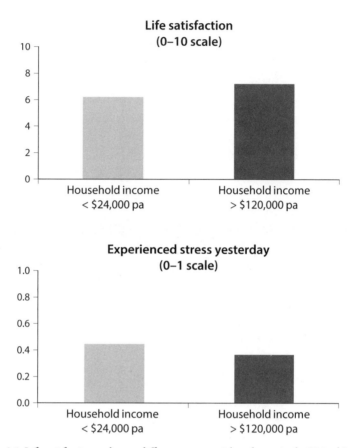

Figure 3.1. Life satisfaction and stress differences across rich and poor in the United States. *Source*: Graham (2016).

Note: Histogram bars indicate the mean response per income category in the Gallup poll and correspond, roughly, to income quintiles 1 and 5. All differences of response means are statistically significant at the 1% level. Life satisfaction is measured by the best possible life (*bpl*). The scale runs from the worst possible life imaginable (0) to the best one (10). Stress yesterday is a simple yes (1) or no (0) response. The 10% difference on the *bpl* question is large and equivalent in life satisfaction terms to moving from Denmark—the happiest country in the world—to Qatar, or, within the United States, of getting a college degree rather than just a high school diploma.

I next compared the United States and Latin America—a region long known for its high levels of inequality, although there has been modest progress in reducing it in recent years. The Gini coefficient for the region as a whole fell from 0.54 in 2002 to 0.47 in 2014 (Gasperini, Cruces, and Tornaralli, 2016). In this instance I used data from the Gallup World Poll for 2005 to 2013, as it has the same survey metrics and time frame for both places.

For evaluative well-being, I again used the BPL question. I used two measures of hedonic well-being, one positive and one negative (as positive and negative affect do not always track together and ideally should be measured separately). For negative affect I used the stress question and for positive affect a question that asks if respondents smiled frequently yesterday (both are yes or no questions, on a 0–1 scale). As a gauge of mobility attitudes, I used a question that asks respondents, "Can people in this country get ahead if they work hard or not?" (with possible answers being yes or no, 1–0).

As above, a simple look at the mean responses for the lowest and highest quintiles for each sample (averaged out for 2006–2013) is telling. Indeed, the scores suggest that the differences between the lives and future outlooks of poor and rich Americans are significantly larger than those between poor and rich Latin Americans (see Table A.1 and Figures 3.2a–3.2d).

The one exception is evaluative well-being, as measured by the BPL question, where levels are higher for the United States than for the Latin American countries. This is not a surprise, as the BPL question introduces a relative component and is most closely correlated with income across both individuals and countries than any of the other evaluative questions (such as life satisfaction and happiness in general). The difference between the average scores of the poorest and richest quintiles in the United States is also marginally smaller than that for LAC, at least in most years, and averaged out over the period (see Table A.1 and Figure 3.2a).

In contrast, on all of the other questions—smiling, stress, and hard work gets you ahead—the difference between the scores of the poor and the rich is significantly smaller in LAC than it is in the United States (see Table A.1 and Figures 3.2b–3.2d). Both of the hedonic metrics—stress and smiling—exhibit a much larger gap between poor and rich Americans than between poor and rich Latin Americans. The hard work variable, meanwhile, tells an even more compelling story. Not only is the gap smaller between Latin

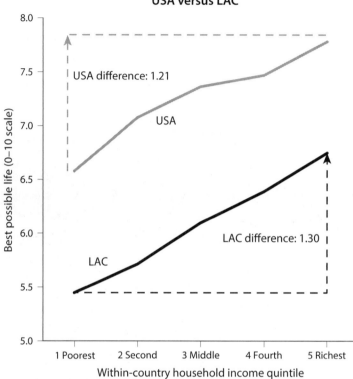

Figure 3.2a. Life satisfaction.
Source: Calculations by Chattopadhyay and Graham, based on the Gallup World Poll, 2006–2013.

American poor and rich quintiles, but in some years the poor actually score higher than the rich.[8]

At least in recent years in Latin America, the poor have much more faith that working hard can get you ahead than the poor in the United States; in other words, they are more likely to live the American Dream. While scores on this variable in the United States are, on average, high compared to most

[8] The trends across quintiles 1 and 5 show a monotonic increase in beliefs in hard work for the United States (with some modest differences across years that average out over the pooled period). The trend is much flatter in Latin America, and displays a very modest downward movement for the middle income quintile.

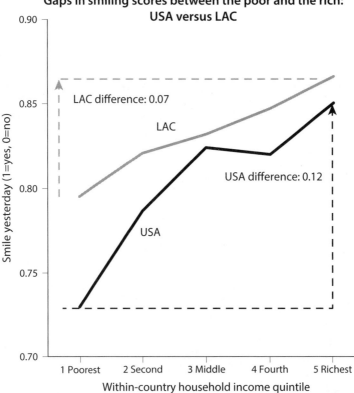

Figure 3.2b. Smiling yesterday.
Source: Calculations by Chattopadhyay and Graham, based on the Gallup World Poll, 2006–2013.
Note: Measured as, did you smile frequently yesterday, yes (1) or no (0)?

countries, what is notable is that the gap between the scores of the rich and the poor in the United States is much larger than it is in Latin America (see Table A.1 and Figure 3.2d). The general picture is one of significant differences in well-being and outlooks for the future between the poor and the rich in the United States, reinforcing the picture of "two Americas" that is described earlier in the chapter from several different perspectives and methodological approaches.

These are simply averages, of course, and may wash out important nuances. I attempted to get a more fine-grained view of the determinants of mobility

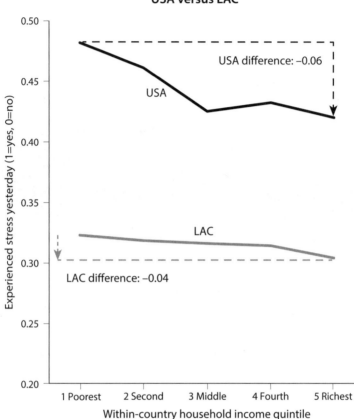

Figure 3.2c. Stress.
Source: Calculations by Chattopadhyay and Graham, based on the Gallup World Poll, 2006–2013.
Note: Measured as, did you experience stress yesterday, yes (1) or no (0)? The poor are defined as those in the bottom income quintile of their country's income distribution and the rich as those in the wealthiest.

attitudes, and ran separate regressions for each sample (United States, LAC), with mobility attitudes (e.g., belief in hard work) as the dependent variable and the usual sociodemographic variables—income, year dummies, country dummies (for the LAC sample), and the BPL and stress questions—as independent variables. As the question is binary (yes/no), I used a logit specification. The baseline equation is:

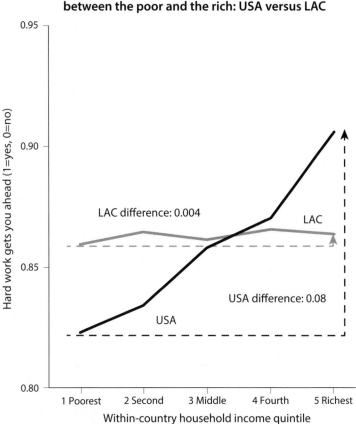

Figure 3.2d. Belief in hard work gets you ahead.
Source: Calculations by Chattopadhyay and Graham, based on the Gallup World Poll, 2006–2013.
Note: Measured as whether or not someone who works hard in this country can get ahead: yes (1) or no (0).

Y_{it}(*hard work Y, for person i, in time period t*)
$= \beta_0 + \beta_1 * (income) + \beta_2 * (vector\ of\ socio - dem\ traits) + \beta_3$
$* (bpl) + \beta_4 * (stress) + (year\ dummies) + (country\ dummies\ for\ LAC$
specification$) + \varepsilon$

The econometric results essentially confirm the patterns in the averages. Most importantly, the coefficient on log income (measured in international dollars, where respondents place themselves in brackets based on their domestic currency, which is then converted into international dollar values) is six times greater for the United States than it is for Latin America. Education plays no role in the United States but is (surprisingly) negatively correlated with hard work beliefs in Latin America (this may have to do with ongoing changes in rewards to different levels of education in the latter). Women are less likely than men to believe that hard work gets you ahead in the United States, but more likely to in Latin America.

And, not surprisingly, innate character traits and attitudes—e.g., natural optimism or pessimism—play a strong role in mobility attitudes in both contexts. Respondents with higher levels of evaluative well-being are more likely to believe in hard work, while those with higher levels of stress are less likely (Table 3.1). As an example of the orders of magnitude, individuals in the United States who are one point higher on the ten-point life satisfaction scale have a 2.3 percent higher probability of believing that hard work can get them ahead, while those who reported experiencing stress the day before have a 2.8 percent lower probability. And an additional unit of (log) income is associated (on average) with a 1.2 percent higher probability of believing that hard work will get respondents ahead. The logarithmic specification highlights the importance of income for those with less of it (at the bottom of the distribution) and, as such, an additional unit of income will have more effect on the beliefs probabilities of those at the distribution, at least in theory.

In addition, to make sure that studying Latin America as a whole was not hiding major differences across countries, I ran our hard work beliefs regressions for six "prototype" countries that reflect different wealth and inequality levels, among other things: Brazil, Chile, Costa Rica, El Salvador, Honduras, and Mexico. There is no clear pattern in the relationship between income and hard work beliefs across countries. Indeed, controlling for positive affect (smiling yesterday), income is positively correlated with hard work beliefs only in Brazil and El Salvador, negatively correlated with them in Chile and Honduras, and insignificant in Costa Rica and Mexico. As such, there is no evidence that particular types of countries are driving our findings for the region as a whole.[9]

---

[9] Regression results are available from the author.

Table 3.1. Probit average marginal effects: Hard work gets one ahead (1 = yes, 0 = no)

	(1)	(2)
Variable	USA	LAC
Age	−0.006***	−0.003***
	(0.002)	(0.000)
Age-squared/100	0.007***	0.003***
	(0.002)	(0.000)
Female	−0.039***	0.013***
	(0.012)	(0.002)
Married	0.004	0.011***
	(0.013)	(0.002)
HS education or beyond	−0.004	−0.020***
	(0.044)	(0.003)
Best possible life (0–10)	0.023***	0.007***
	(0.003)	(0.000)
Experienced stress yesterday	−0.028**	−0.029***
	(0.012)	(0.002)
Log(household income, in international $)	0.012*	0.002*
	(0.007)	(0.001)
Controls		
Year dummy variables (base: 2013)	Yes	Yes
Country dummy variables (base: Argentina)	No	Yes
Observations	4,960	122,331

Source: Data from Gallup World Poll 2006–2014.
Note: Robust standard errors in parentheses.
*$p < .1.$ **$p < .05.$ ***$p < .01.$

How Does the Distribution of Hard Work Beliefs Compare in Other Regions?

While there are many cultural similarities between Americans and Latin Americans, it is plausible (although not likely) that the difference in their hard work beliefs distribution has to do with Latin Americans being, on average, poorer, and therefore having more margin to get ahead. Thus I compared the patterns in the United States and LAC with those in Europe, as well as with a selection of countries in Southeast Asia.

The Eurozone-16 group of countries, which excludes the Baltic countries, comprises the European countries that are most like the United States: Austria, Belgium, Cyprus, Finland, France, Germany, Greece, Ireland, Italy, Luxembourg, Malta, the Netherlands, Portugal, Slovakia, Slovenia, and Spain. The Eurozone countries are similar to the United States in terms of per capita levels of income, on average, although they also typically have significantly lower levels of inequality than the United States or Latin America. Gini coefficients range from mid-30s (0.35) in the most unequal countries, such as Spain (0.34) and Portugal (0.34), to the low 20s (0.23) in the more equal ones, such as Slovenia (0.23) and Slovakia (0.25). (For a summary of distributive trends in recent years in the Eurozone, see Wolfe [2013].)

Overall, the levels of belief in hard work in the Eurozone are lower than those in either the United States or LAC (see Figure 3.3). This may in part be because of the more extensive social safety nets and welfare programs in Europe, which in turn reflect a stronger and long-held belief in the role of the collective, as well as individual effort, in sustaining societies. Yet the distribution of hard work beliefs in Europe falls somewhere in between the United States and LAC. While these beliefs are not as equally shared across poor and rich in Europe as they are in LAC, they are more equally shared than they are in the United States. Still, it is notable that the U.S. poor are more likely to have faith in hard work than are the rich in the Eurozone-16.

We also looked at each country individually, to make sure that the findings were not driven by a particular country. While average levels of support for hard work range from a low of 0.56/0.57 in Slovakia and Slovenia, respectively, to a high of 0.89 in the Netherlands and 0.91 in Luxembourg, the distribution of beliefs across quintiles in all of the countries is remarkably flat, with the most unequal distribution by far in Slovakia. Thus differences across countries in the Eurozone are much greater than differences across socioeconomic cohorts.

We also compared attitudes in the United States and LAC with those in Asia, a region well known for its strong individual work ethic, but that is also very diverse and quite different from the United States. The countries in Southeast Asia for which we have World Poll data are China, Indonesia, Japan, Korea, Laos, Malaysia, Mongolia, Myanmar, the Philippines, Thailand, and Vietnam. Southeast Asia as a whole is not a particularly unequal region. Some countries such as Japan, Laos, and Vietnam have rather low

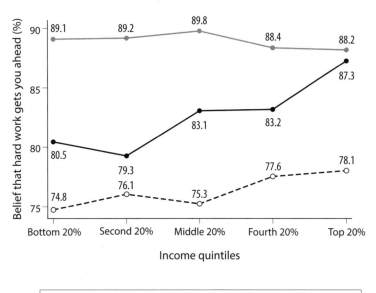

Figure 3.3. Hard work gets you ahead: Eurozone-16 countries, United States, and Latin America.
Source: Author's calculations based on Gallup World Poll, 2006–2013.
Note: The region averages are not weighted by country size.

Gini coefficients (ranging from 0.32 to 0.34—the low coefficients for the latter two are not surprising as they are former transition economies). Some of the poorer developing economies, such as Thailand and the Philippines, demonstrate higher levels of inequality (0.41 and 0.44 respectively), as does China (0.41). Increases in inequality from very low to relatively high levels were part and parcel of China's transition and growth boom in the 1990s and early 2000s, and are believed to be part of the cause of the sharp declines in life satisfaction at precisely the time that growth took off (Easterlin et al., 2012; Graham, Zhou, and Zhang, 2015).

Average levels of hard work beliefs demonstrate large differences across Japan and Korea on the one hand, and the rest of the region on the other. The average scores for China and Asia as a whole are very high and quite evenly distributed. Indeed, rather remarkably, mean hard work beliefs are on average slightly higher for the poor than for the rich. In contrast, average scores for both Korea and Japan are low and also quite different across the poor and the rich. For Korea, which has higher scores than Japan, the poor demonstrate the highest scores, they drop down in the middle, and then recoup somewhat for the wealthiest quintile. Japan resembles the United States in terms of trends, with the lowest scores among the poor and the highest among the rich, although Japan's levels of hard work beliefs are significantly lower than those for either the United States or Latin America (see Figure A.1).

In terms of the distribution of beliefs, the most evenly shared hard work beliefs are in Latin America, Southeast Asia as a whole, and China in particular. The United States has large gaps across income cohorts, but Japan and Korea have even larger ones. Korea demonstrates the most optimism among the poor compared to the rest of the distribution, meanwhile, than any of the countries/regions in the comparison. In regression analysis comparing the United States to the three countries that have the most comparable income levels—Japan, Korea, and China—we find, again, that the United States stands out as having the strongest relationship between income levels and hard work beliefs.[10]

Hard Work Beliefs in the Well-Being Distribution

Some of my newest work, with Milena Nikolova, is based on where respondents are in the well-being distribution and their associated behaviors. It confirms this generally positive link between well-being, health, and productivity, on average. Yet we also find that respondents at the very top end of the well-being distribution (e.g., the happiest) diverge a bit, and value full-time employment and income less than the average, but learning and creativity more (Graham and Nikolova, 2015).

---

[10] As in the case of the United States and Latin America, I ran a (logit) regression with hard work beliefs as the dependent variable, including the usual sociodemographic and economic controls as well as year dummies on the right-hand side. Income is insignificant in Southeast Asia, as in the case of Latin America, using two separate specifications: income quintiles (with the poorest being the reference group) and log income. When I looked at individual countries in the region separately, I found some differences in the role of income but no consistent or logical pattern. Given the very large differences in relationship between beliefs and income distributions across the individual countries, this is not a great surprise.

As also noted in Chapter 1, related work by Binder and Coad (2015) finds that those respondents in the highest well-being/life satisfaction quantile suffer much less (in well-being terms) from being unemployed than do those in the least happy quantile. They also find distinct differences when they use markers of mental well-being rather than life satisfaction, with smaller differences between those in the lowest and highest well-being categories than those in the lowest and highest life satisfaction categories. It is important to reiterate that negative affect/moods and depression are not the direct analogue/opposite of high levels of life satisfaction, and that the depressed have distinct negative traits and the happiest have distinct positive ones.

In a twist on this and building on the above research on hard work beliefs, we used quantile regressions to examine the correlation between well-being and mobility beliefs according to where in the well-being distribution respondents are. We followed the method in Binder and Coad (2011) and Koenker and Bassett (1978). While standard regressions describe the conditional mean, quantile regressions allow us to explore the entire conditional distribution by analyzing the effects of the covariates at different points of the well-being distribution. In essence, they work like ordinary least squares (OLS), but instead of minimizing the sum of squared residuals, they minimize the sum of equally weighted absolute residuals (for the median), and the sum of differentially weighted residuals for the other quantiles.

We again compared the United States and Latin America and found important differences across the two regions. For the U.S. sample, the coefficient on belief in hard work falls monotonically from the least happy quantile (where it is highest) to the happiest quantile, where it loses significance (Table A.2). In terms of orders of magnitude, those in the least happy quantile who believe in hard work are 0.8 points higher on the ten-point life satisfaction scale than are those who do not, while there is no difference in the life satisfaction scores of those who believe in hard work and those who do not for respondents who are in the happiest quantile (e.g., already very happy).

In contrast, in Latin America, the coefficient is roughly the same across well-being quantiles, although slightly lower for the happiest quantile and the highest for the middle one (Table A.3). As such, belief in hard work seems to be equally important to life satisfaction across the board in LAC. We noted above that hard work beliefs were more equally shared across income quintiles in LAC than in the United States. We find here, in addition, that they are also more equally shared across well-being quantiles in LAC than in the United States.

Thus belief in hard work is most important for the least happy Americans, and not particularly important to the happiest, who are likely to be happy regardless. Another way to interpret these findings is that if you are in the unhappy part of the distribution in America, believing in hard work and the future makes a positive contribution (perhaps by providing some hope). There may be an intertemporal dimension to these findings, particularly for the United States where the financial crisis was very stark. Both subjective well-being and hard work beliefs moved over time across the period, with some differences across cohorts.

From 2006 to 2013, both subjective well-being and hard work beliefs moved up for the very poorest quintile, but moved down slightly for quintile 2. The latter is a cohort that is more likely to be in the labor force and therefore was more exposed to recession-related unemployment and other associated losses that are emblematic of the hollowing out of the middle class. The wealthiest cohorts (quintile 5), meanwhile, experienced a clear drop in subjective well-being at the time of the onset of the 2008–2009 crisis, and then a sharp recovery thereafter, in contrast to those in quintile 2, who likely experienced employment or other shocks in the crisis and remained vulnerable even in the recovery (see Figure 3.4).

Thus it is possible that some of those respondents in the lowest subjective well-being quantile were temporarily there, and their belief in hard work was a signal that they were hoping for better times. The downward trend in subjective well-being for those in the near poor income quintile, meanwhile, mirrors the economic fate that those same respondents are likely to have had in the postcrisis period. The intertemporal component of this is a work in progress, and we hope to answer these questions more fully going forward.

Conclusions

For decades a broadly shared belief that individuals who worked hard would find opportunities and get ahead was part and parcel of American national pride and culture, an explanation for its dynamic economy, and an explanation for the unusually high tolerance for inequality. That shared belief, in

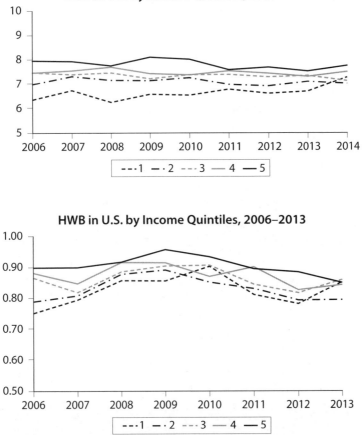

Figure 3.4. Subjective well-being and hard work belief in the United States by income quintiles across time.
Source: Author's calculations based on Gallup Healthways Poll, 2006–2013.
Note: The top/wealthiest quintile is 5.

turn, hinged on a relationship between beliefs and behavior: that people who believed in their future would work hard and invest in the future. A nascent body of well-being literature supports the proposition that most individuals who are optimistic about the future tend to also invest in those futures and, in turn, have better than average future outcomes.

The effects of inequality on individual well-being, meanwhile, are mediated by what it signals for the future. If it is seen as a sign of potential opportunities and rewards to individual efforts, then it has positive effects on well-being and seems to be part of a virtuous beliefs cycle. If it signals persistent advantages for some cohorts and disadvantages for others, however, it tends to have negative effects on well-being and can feed into a negative beliefs cycle, where even talented or educated individuals do not believe they can get ahead, either because the deck is stacked against them or because their identification with a disadvantaged group or cohort leads them to believe that they have less ability.

Not coincidentally, at the same time that inequality has increased markedly in the United States and mobility rates are proving to be lower than in many other OECD economies, there is evidence that the American Dream is also very unevenly shared across socioeconomic cohorts. The poor and the rich in the United States lead very different lives, with the former having a much harder time looking beyond day-to-day struggles and associated high levels of stress, and the latter able to pursue much better futures for themselves and for their children, with the gaps between the two likely to increase even more in the future, for the many reasons discussed in this chapter. As such, perhaps it should be no surprise that beliefs in the future and in the role of hard work are very different across these cohorts.

What is surprising is how large the beliefs gap is, both in terms of absolute size and in terms of its size relative to that of other countries and regions, particularly Latin America, a region long known for its high levels of poverty and inequality. The gaps in belief in hard work, in experiencing daily stress, and in measures of positive affect are all much greater across the poor and the rich in the United States than they are in Latin America. And the gaps are the greatest in hard work beliefs, precisely the marker that best captures belief in the American Dream. Income levels are a key determinant of hard work beliefs in the United States; in contrast income levels do not matter at all to believing in hard work in Latin America. The distribution of beliefs across poor and rich cohorts is also more equally shared in both Europe and South Asia than it is in the United States.

We also looked at variance across the well-being distribution. We found that believing in hard work had a strong positive correlation with life satisfaction for the least happy cohorts in the United States—perhaps because it is one source of hope, or perhaps because the respondents were only temporarily unhappy due to a negative economic or other shock and thus only temporarily in the least happy quantile.

Over the period under study, the wealthiest respondents had a temporary dip in life satisfaction during the crisis, but then recovered. In contrast the near poor (those in income quintile 2) had a steady decline in life satisfaction and no recovery. The economic crisis likely accentuated the effects of longer term drivers of inequality of well-being, such as the increasing vulnerability of those in or near the middle class, the increasing distance between their incomes and those the top of the distribution.

In general, the gaps in important markers of well-being and in beliefs about the future are notably large in the United States compared to other regions, despite its reputation as the land of opportunity. A great deal of evidence, much of it reviewed in this chapter, suggests that individuals with higher levels of well-being have better future outcomes, both because of the role of a number of factors associated with well-being, such as good health, and because higher levels of well-being are associated with more faith in the future—and therefore greater likelihood of investing in it. This suggests that the gaps between the outcomes of the rich and the poor may well increase in the future, a possibility that I explore in greater detail in the following two chapters.

CHAPTER 4

The High Costs of Being Poor in the Land of the Dream

Stress, Insecurity, and Lack of Hope

When you are forever fighting a degenerating sense of "nobodiness"—then you will understand why we find it difficult to wait. There comes a time when the cup of endurance runs over, and men are no longer willing to be plunged into the abyss of despair.

—Martin Luther King, Jr., Why We Can't Wait

Decades ago my father, a pediatrician at Johns Hopkins, published an article in the Archives of Environmental Health titled "The High Costs of Being Poor" (Adrianzen and Graham, 1974). He and his coauthor documented how much more the urban poor in Peru paid for water, which they purchased from trucks, and electricity, for which they substituted candles and kerosene, than did the rich, who had access in their homes. The poor paid roughly fifteen times more per unit cost, even though the services were of much lower quality. His research highlighted linkages between this regressive pricing (controlling for other factors) and the inferior health and nutrition outcomes of the children of parents without access to piped water and electricity.

Today the same urban slums where he (and later I) conducted research now have water, electricity, paved streets, and a growing middle class, and infant malnutrition is virtually nonexistent (if anything, obesity is becoming a concern). Meanwhile, in the United States, there are broad concerns about the hollowing out of the middle class, the stagnation of incomes at the bottom, and uneven access to opportunity—which is the foundation of the American Dream.

The high costs of being poor in the United States are less about basic material goods such as water and electricity than about access to the opportunities that typically come with being middle class, and the high costs of insecurity that are associated with being poor. Health insurance, decent quality education, and even modest financial buffers are key factors that allow individuals to move beyond the daily struggles associated with poverty, including stigma and discrimination. Trends in well-being and in attitudes about hard work reflect these changing realities. These attitudes and related behaviors and expectations are often passed on from parents to children, analogous to the long-term health costs that children in the Peruvian slums used to suffer.

The United States has traditionally been an outlier in terms of its high tolerance for inequality and widely held public belief in individual effort and opportunity, including among the poor. Yet that belief is being eroded, particularly among the poorest, as the data shown throughout the book demonstrate quite starkly. At the same time, our analysis below highlights important differences across poor cohorts, some of which provide glimmers of hope.

The discussion in Chapter 3 highlighted how attitudes about the merits of hard work are more evenly shared across the poor and the rich in Latin America than they are in the United States. Average reported stress levels, meanwhile, are higher in the United States than in Latin America, and the gap between the levels of the rich and poor is much greater, with the U.S. poor reporting the highest levels of stress of all cohorts. High levels of stress are generally correlated with an inability to plan ahead, lower life satisfaction levels, and worse health outcomes.

Our research, based on the Gallup Healthways data for the United States and discussed below, shows that higher levels of income not only provide the means to pursue opportunities and fulfilling lives but also mediate the negative effects of stress. "Good" stress seems to be associated with goal pursuit. "Bad" stress, associated with struggles and uncertainty, is more common at the bottom of the distribution, and is associated with higher levels of suffering in general.

Based on the same data, we also find that pain, worry, sadness, and anger (reported as experienced the day before or not) are all significantly higher among low-income cohorts than among wealthy ones, while reported satisfaction with life as a whole is significantly lower (see Figure 4.1 and Figures 3.2a and 3.2c). Similarly, a study by Ronald Anderson (2014) finds a big difference in reports of chronic suffering across income groups, based on data from the 2010 Integrated National Health Interview Study. Of U.S. respondents, 64 percent were free of suffering. Yet those with incomes below the poverty line were twice as likely to report chronic pain and mental distress than those earning $75,000 or more, and three to five times more likely to have extreme pain or extreme distress.

Experiencing discrimination—which is more common for the poor than the rich, particularly if they are the recipients of government transfers—is also associated with stress and with lower levels of life satisfaction (Swenson, 2015). Among other things, discrimination raises the transaction costs of simple things such as getting a loan or buying a home. A recent study by Thayer and Kuzawa (2015) finds that maternal stress related to discrimination is associated with lower birth weights—which are linked to worse outcomes on a number of progress indicators—thus passing disadvantage on to the next generation.

This chapter focuses on why there are additional costs to being poor—above and beyond the well-known, objective obstacles to upward mobility—which show up in hope, expectations for the future, and attitudes about hard work. These create an additional vicious (and intergenerational) circle that contributes to the high costs of being poor in a wealthy land known for its mobility dreams. In our analysis, we explore trends in optimism about the future across different socioeconomic and racial cohorts, as well as the potential roles of stress and of local level inequality. Stress can make it very difficult for the poor to plan for the future, and high inequality can make "success" seem even further out of their reach.

Markers of Poverty in the United States

What is it about being poor that makes it so hard to get ahead? What is different about being poor in the United States than in other countries? The poor in the United States are not as materially deprived and have much higher levels of income, on average, than their counterparts in many other countries, as noted above. And, depending on where they live, they have access to a wide range of public goods that the destitute in poorer countries typically do not have.

Yet the U.S. poor score lower than those in many countries in terms of objective indicators of health, such as life expectancy, obesity rates, and cardiovascular disease. Some of these markers—obesity in particular—are in turn linked to lower rates of social mobility later in life (Gortmaker et al., 1993). And they also score much lower on subjective measures, such as stress levels and attitudes about hard work and the future. As Chapter 3 highlights, the U.S. poor score significantly lower than their counterparts in Latin America, a much poorer region, on all of these subjective markers. These low expectations and high levels of stress, meanwhile, seem to play out in a number of vicious circles, including in the objective health indicators. Higher discount rates and impatience, for example, are associated with much higher probabilities of being obese (Courtemanche, Heutel, and McAlvanah, 2014).

If it is not for the most part material deprivation alone that makes it harder for people to escape poverty, what are the significant markers of being poor in the United States? An important one is high levels of stress, which are, in turn, associated with insecurity, daily struggles, short time horizons, and lack of ability to plan ahead. These factors then act as a disincentive to make investments in the future (in terms of savings, health, and education, among others). They can even discourage the acceptance of available opportunities, such as in the case of Barofsky's (2015) work on the take-up of health insurance under the Affordable Care Act (ACA) expansion. He finds that take-up levels of the ACA expansion by the poor (including those who report having health problems) vary according to discount rates and ability to plan for the future (discussed in detail Chapter 5).

There are, meanwhile, significant numbers of poor in the United States—roughly 1.5 million families—who do face material deprivation, and live on as little as $2 per day (Edin and Shaefer, 2015; Keiger, 2015b). They typically have precarious and unstable jobs and a range of household- and individual-level challenges, ranging from single parenthood to depression, stress, and addiction. They tend to be what sociologists call "disconnected": neither working nor receiving welfare. This group of extreme poor fall well below the official U.S. poverty line of $20,090 for a family of three, or roughly $18 per day. For this group, it is not difficult to imagine that the problems of low

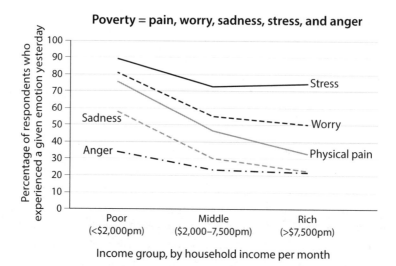

Figure 4.1. Manifestations of poverty in the United States.
Source: Chattopadhyay and Graham calculations based on Gallup data for 2008–2013.

expectations, short time horizons, and constant insecurity are an order of magnitude greater than those for other low-income cohorts.

As indicated above, pain, worry, and anger—all markers of ill-being—are also higher among the poor than among other cohorts in the United States (see Figure 4.1). Some of these markers are, no doubt, simply associated with the objective markers of being poor: dangerous neighborhoods and poor-quality schools and hospitals, lack of health insurance, unstable employment and working hours, racial and other kinds of discrimination, and high rates of single-parent households and unplanned pregnancy. These factors alone can explain a loss of personal efficacy among the poor, as Putnam (2015) highlights. Recent findings on mortality rates among uneducated whites (discussed in detail below), and in particular the roles of suicide and drug and alcohol addiction, which in turn highlight deep desperation, are a case in point.

Yet some of this desperation may also be related to the difficulties of being poor in a country where the very visible lifestyles of the wealthy are increasingly out of reach. Michael Marmot and Richard Wilkinson (2006) have (famously and not without controversy) highlighted negative inequality and health outcome channels in their work on the social determinants of health. Marmot et al.'s (1991) early findings on the worse health outcomes and lower life expectancy among low-status compared to high-status British civil servants are still widely cited today, for example.

The visibility of inequality seems to play a role in this channel, as in the case of the civil servants. Recent experimental work suggests that seeing wealth that is beyond one's reach seems to be corrosive to trust, cooperation, and a sense of a commonly shared public good, as discussed in Chapter 3 (Nishi et al., 2015). Oyserman's work (2013), meanwhile, shows how distance between what is achievable and what is considered to be success can undermine the efforts and expectations of students from poor backgrounds, even in highly rated colleges. And constantly being in a low pay/low rewards group can lead to differential beliefs about ability and to persistently low expectations, as Jeff Butler's (2014) experimental work shows.

Location also seems to matter a great deal to the nature and persistence of U.S. poverty, and there has been increasing attention to the role of place (for an early example, see Ludwig et al., 2012). Chetty et al.'s (2014, 2015) work on the Moving to Opportunity (MTO) experiment suggests that where and when poor children move to better locations makes a very large difference on children's outcomes. Yet the initial evaluations of MTO found effects only on the mental health and happiness of poor mothers, which in and of themselves are positive and may have provided a positive hope channel.

While the early studies did not have a long enough time frame to assess children's outcomes (Ludwig et al., 2012), the more recent work by Chetty and coauthors finds that place also matters in terms of college attendance, earnings, and marriage rates (all markers of exiting poverty). And the age that children moved was very relevant. If children moved to better neighborhoods before age thirteen, the effects of moving were much more positive for long-term outcomes (increased annual incomes of 31 percent by the mid-twenties, 2 percent higher marriage rates, and 2.5 percent higher college attendance rates), with the differences showing up even among the same families. The younger siblings who moved at the same time did much better than their older siblings.

The places that were markers of success had better elementary schools, a higher share of two-parent families, greater involvement in civic and religious groups, and more residential integration across socioeconomic groups. In contrast, the places where the program was less successful had more inequality in income and housing costs and more segregation. The former makes it difficult for the poor to afford to integrate, while racial segregation is an obvious additional barrier. The MTO research suggests that if poor children are removed from the markers of poverty and ill-being and relocated to places where success is within their reach, they are more likely to succeed.

While the MTO studies did not explicitly assess the effects of mother's mental health on children's outcomes, it is not much of a stretch of the imagination to posit that it had a role. Very recent work by Magdalena Bendini (2015), based on the Young Lives survey of children born in the millennium in Peru and followed over time since then, explicitly assesses the effects of reported maternal depression on children's outcomes. She finds a modest positive effect of mother's mental health on both growth outcomes and learning scores. While it is difficult to definitively establish causality (as difficult or disadvantaged children can also affect maternal mental health), this is another example of an instance where hope seems to matter, in addition to objective conditions.

An increasing body of research cites the importance of "soft skills," in addition to formal education, in determining children's success later in life (see, for example, Putnam, 2015, and also the discussion in Chapter 3 of differences in these skills across SES status as found by Shanahan and colleagues, 2014). These include skills such as strong work habits, self-discipline, teamwork, leadership, and a sense of civic engagement, and are acquired both in the classroom and via extracurricular activities (which are much less available to and affordable for the poor in general). There are also gaps in terms of access to soft skills in the classroom for low-income children. Joanna Venator and Richard Reeves (2015a), using data from the 2010 National Longitudinal Survey of Youth, find that children in the bottom quintile are more than twice as likely as those in the top quintile to report that they are rarely/never given a writing assignment or asked to work together in small groups, for example. Putnam (2015), meanwhile, documents very large gaps between poor and rich children in the access to extracurricular activities, ranging from sports to music lessons.

Expectations—which are part and parcel of the soft skills story—play a role. Living in "bad" places, with high levels of segregation and inequality, unequally shared public goods, and associated disfunctionality in families and neighborhoods, makes "success" seem unachievable and reinforces the vicious circle of high insecurity, high stress, and high discount rates.

Barofsky's (2015) work, mentioned in Chapter 3, on lack of take-up of available health insurance by respondents with high discount rates is one example. Another is work cited by Richard Reeves on contraception take-up among the poor (Venator and Reeves, 2015b). Even though low-income women say they would be upset about becoming pregnant, they are much less likely to use contraception and to have abortions (in part but not only because of the costs of uninsured abortion; likely also because of education differences and social norms).

Obesity rates are also significantly higher among low-income cohorts. Even though information on healthy living and poor diet are widely available across socioeconomic cohorts, they are largely ignored by some. In part this is due to the difficulties of finding healthy foods (and their costs) and the time and space to exercise in poor neighborhoods; but in part it is the same low expectations/high discount rate story, with expectations and behaviors being passed on from parents to children (Drewnowski and Specter, 2004). Indeed, my own research finds that the stigma associated with being obese (as assessed by the subjective well-being costs and controlling for other factors) is much lower in high-obesity, low-income and racial cohorts where obesity is much more likely to be the norm (Graham, 2008).

There is also stigma associated with being poor in the United States, which is different from other contexts and particularly those with more inclusive social welfare systems. In theory, the increased levels of income from social welfare transfers should boost well-being, particularly for those at the lowest levels of income, by reducing hardship and insecurity. Yet being a transfer recipient in the United States is associated with significant negative well-being costs.

Kendall Swenson (2015) explored the linkages between life satisfaction and receiving assistance, from both public (means-tested transfers) and private sources (family and charitable assistance) in the United States, based on data from the Panel Study of Income Dynamics. He found that recipients of transfers—from all sources—reported lower levels of life satisfaction than nonrecipients, controlling for income and other sociodemographic traits. One explanation for the findings is the stigma attached to receiving means-tested welfare assistance in the United States, unlike many other countries where such assistance is considered a universal benefit. And relying on transfers is a means to compensate for unstable or low-paying work or other circumstances beyond individuals' control, uncertainty that is typically associated with high levels of stress and other markers of ill-being.

It is possible that in a country where individual success is such a focus, those who are not self-sufficient feel less self-worth and purpose. The unemployed are typically much less satisfied with their lives than the average (controlling for income), and these effects are stronger in places where unemployment is less common and support for unemployment benefits is lower, as in the United States (Clark and Oswald, 1994; Stutzer and Lalive, 2004). In addition, the bureaucracies surrounding means-tested programs are less user-friendly than those surrounding universal programs such as Medicare and Social Security, and recipients of transfers encounter various challenges associated with having to interact with social service agencies, including stigma.

Edin and Shaefer (2015), meanwhile, highlight another manner in which the recipients of means-tested programs are treated harshly: the very high penalties that are associated with violations in these programs, such as selling food stamps for cash (which the recipients often need more than food). They note that "under federal sentencing guidelines, penalties for food stamp fraud are more severe than voluntary manslaughter, aggravated assault with a fire-arm, or sexual contact with a child under twelve." They contrast this with the earned income tax credit (EITC) program, which gives tax credits to those with full-time jobs. "This citizenship-enhancing feature of the EITC is like policy magic." The problem, though, is that while EITC is very effective for those with relatively stable employment, it does not apply to the very poorest with precarious and unstable employment. And while the EITC has been very successful, the changes that accompanied the 1996 welfare reform legislation also made it more difficult for this particular group to get other benefits, such as Temporary Assistance for Needy Families (TANF).

More surprising, given the strong skepticism about government assistance that is pervasive in public debates today, Swenson finds that the negative effects of receiving private transfers were just as prevalent as those of receiving public transfers. While the data do not provide the reasons for this finding, it may be that private transfers come with more conditions attached and/or are more unpredictable.

An important caveat is that the negative association between income assistance and life satisfaction does not prove the former reduces overall well-being. It is possible that the low-income families who are able to obtain

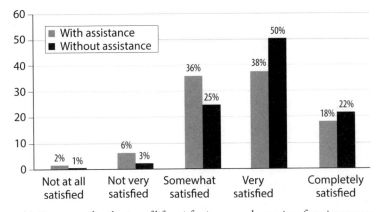

Figure 4.2. Percentage distribution of life satisfaction scores by receipt of any income assistance during the previous year.
Source: Swenson (2015).

enough resources to avoid income assistance have higher life satisfaction scores, but lower well-being outcomes in other areas of their lives (including markers such as stress), than families that receive assistance. And some individuals may feel less positive about their lives when they receive assistance, but seek it in order to provide basic necessities to their families. It is possible that the transfer programs improve the well-being of children but reduce the life satisfaction of the breadwinning adults who answer the surveys.

In addition, people who receive income assistance may have health and other disadvantages that are not observed in the data. Many contend with the poverty-related markers that are cited above: domestic violence, substance abuse, low aptitude, disabilities, discrimination, incarceration, and poor neighborhood conditions, among other challenges. Still, a simple look (in Figure 4.2) at the difference between the life satisfaction responses of those who are and are not recipients of transfers is suggestive.

This figure does not control for intervening factors, such as income and health, and instead highlights the raw distribution of well-being and how it links to transfers. Transfer recipients are disproportionately represented in the lowest life satisfaction categories, suggesting an additional low well-being/transfers pattern (above and beyond the known income channels), which fits into the vicious circle that we have identified elsewhere: low well-being, less likelihood of investing in the future, and worse outcomes, including across generations. (Causality likely runs in two directions: from environmental challenges—including reliance on transfers—to low levels of well-being, and from low levels of well-being to worse outcomes and the need to rely on transfers.)

Swenson (2015) also finds that the negative coefficient on receipt of transfers is less statistically robust for respondents in the lowest income quintile than for those in higher quintiles. The most destitute families may experience hardship such that the benefits of assistance counter stigma effects. The challenges associated with very deep poverty and the stress related to difficulties in obtaining basic necessities consumes energy and cognitive functioning to a degree that other priorities—including planning for the future—are set aside. Struggles with unpredictable hours and child care arrangements as well as the unpleasant nature of poor-quality, menial jobs may far outweigh concerns about stigma.

In contrast, those who are higher up in the distribution may be relying on assistance to overcome a temporary negative shock (such as unemployment). They may feel more stigma from having to fall back on assistance (private or public), as it is less common for their socioeconomic or professional reference group. They may also fall into the category of the "hollowing out" middle class, who face increasing insecurity and reported lower levels of well-being than the poorest during the financial crisis, for example (discussed in Chapter 3).

Despite the myth of increasing numbers of people relying on welfare, which often characterizes the public discussion, as well as the extent to which it disproportionately benefits minorities, the number of recipients on TANF has been falling over time. While this varies across states, the trend is uniformly negative. And the distribution of who benefits from TANF is also fairly even across racial cohorts. In 2014, the breakdown of TANF recipients was 27.1 percent white, 30.5 percent black, and 36.8 percent Hispanic (Trisi, 2016). Decreasing levels of support for redistributive spending among blacks, meanwhile, as highlighted by Kuziemko et al. (2015), suggest a gradual change in fortunes that is echoed in the findings on poor black optimism and poor white pessimism below.

These findings highlight the costs of being poor in a country where individual success is universally applauded and public support for those who fall behind is regarded with deep skepticism. As Robert Putnam (2015) writes in his recent book, this reflects the extent to which we have "privatized risk" rather than recognizing the collective benefits of helping the poor—and their children—catch up. Along these same lines, a recent study of support for redistribution in the United States (cited in Chapter 1) found that public support for universal programs for the working poor—such as minimum wage and EITC—was much higher than support for transfer programs (Kuziemko et al., 2015).

In sharp contrast to the United States, many Latin American countries have reduced poverty and inequality in recent years through nonstigmatizing income support, which hinges on recipients investing in their futures: enrolling their children in school and receiving preventive health care (Lustig, Pessino, and Scott, 2013). In the United States, initiatives such as early childhood education, home visiting programs, and better coordination of existing services have insufficient support and resources.

Our work discussed in Chapter 3, on how hard work beliefs differ depending on where in the well-being distribution people are, is relevant here. Some people are trapped in low-well-being, low-income, and low-expectations circles and in persistent poverty. Others, meanwhile, seem to continue to believe in hard work and that belief mediates low levels of life satisfaction, presumably by providing some hope for the future. Some of this may relate to being temporarily rather than permanently in poverty.

It is also important to note that low-expectation, low-well-being poverty traps can be manipulated or changed via interventions, even simple ones. The work by Hall and colleagues on affirmation interventions and task performance in soup kitchens that I discuss in Chapter 5 is suggestive, as is that by Mullainathan and colleagues on providing the very poor with a productive asset—and hope—in developing country settings. This is clearly a potential positive channel that I will be exploring explicitly in future research.

Who Believes in the Future in the Land of the Dream? Some Original Empirical Analysis

Given the above discussion and the focus in Chapter 3 on the state of beliefs in hard work getting one ahead in the United States compared to other places, a central question is what drives hope and expectations for the future.

Does it vary with respondents' levels of income and/or according to other sociodemographic traits? Does it vary across places and levels of inequality?

In the following section, I focus on differential attitudes about the future across socioeconomic and racial cohorts, and the extent to which they are mediated by the conditions in which different cohorts live, ranging from poverty to stress to local levels of inequality. A wide body of research, which is reviewed in detail in Chapter 5, suggests that these attitudes matter to behavioral outcomes. Individuals with very limited means are often consumed by daily experience and the associated stress and, as a result, have less capacity to craft and invest in their futures, as well as less confidence that those investments will pay off. I also focus on the role of inequality, as it can contribute to low expectations by making "success" seem unattainable. While I find evidence of these vicious circles, I also find major differences in attitudes about the future across poor cohorts, with some having much more hope and resilience than others.

For the analysis here, I rely on a variable that is in both the Gallup World and Gallup Healthways data, and is a gauge of optimism about the future (among other things).[1] It immediately follows the best possible life (BPL) question in the survey and uses the same ten-step ladder as a scale, but asks respondents where they think they will be on the BPL ladder in five years (as opposed to where they are today). The BPL future question is more speculative than BPL present and, as such, is more influenced by innate optimism.

I began by looking at the simple correlation coefficient between the future BPL question and hard work beliefs for the United States, for LAC, and for the world as a whole. The two variables are positively correlated in general, which is not a surprise. Yet they are far from perfectly correlated, suggesting that there are many other intervening factors in the determinants of each and, as noted above, that the latter is a bit more speculative. For the worldwide sample, hard work beliefs and the future BPL correlate at .154. The correlation for the United States alone is similar, at .142, and for LAC it is slightly lower, at .086.

---

[1] The hard work beliefs question that I used in Chapter 3 to compare the United States and Latin America is only in the World Poll and not in the U.S. Healthways. As such, I was not able to explore it in the detail required here to analyze variance across races and other demographic traits.

One reason for the relatively low strength of the correlation is that the future BPL question likely captures innate optimism in addition to realistic assessments about the future more than does the hard work question, which is more framed by its emphasis on work. In previous research comparing regions around the world, Milena Nikolova and I (Graham and Nikolova, 2015) found that innate optimism played more of a role in explaining a range of well-being trends in Latin America than it does in most other regions, which, in part, helps explain why Latin American countries typically score higher in worldwide comparisons of average country life satisfaction and GDP per capita than most other countries at comparable income levels.

In collaboration with Sergio Pinto, I then explored the determinants of hope for the future (via this future life satisfaction question [BPLfut]) for the United States in greater detail, based on the Gallup Healthways data. As BPLfut is on an ordinal ten-point scale that approximates cardinality (as does the original ladder question), we began with an ordered logit specification and then ran an OLS regression. Given the similarity of the coefficients across the two specifications, we used the latter results for ease of interpretation.

We began by comparing the correlates of BPLfut in the United States, to see the extent to which (if any) they differed from those for present-day BPL. We first ran BPL as the dependent variable, with the usual controls, and then the same specification with BPLfut as the dependent variable. Given our interest in possible present bias among some disadvantaged cohorts, we looked in detail across income and racial cohorts, based on the more detailed and larger Gallup Healthways data set. In this data set respondents selected into one of five racial categories: white, black, Hispanic, Asian, and other (which includes Native Americans). Whites make up 84 percent of the sample, blacks 8 percent, Hispanics 3 percent, Asians 1 percent, and other 4 percent; notably minorities are undersampled in the poll. The definitions of racial cohorts changed in the survey in 2011, creating comparability problems across the later years. Given our focus on race cohorts in these regressions, we use the data for 2008 to 2010 only (although the results are almost identical when we use the full sample).[2]

---

[2] The race categories will be consolidated in the 2014 data, and then we will be able to update our analysis, but not in time for this book.

We included these categories in our regressions, as well as interaction terms for being poor or rich and white, poor or rich and black, and poor or rich and Hispanic. The poor were defined as respondents living in households with less than $2,000 per month of income (roughly 20 percent of the sample, and at an income level that corresponds roughly to the official U.S. poverty line for a household of four), while the rich were those respondents living in the top income category of the sample (above $10,000 per month and approximately 15 percent of the sample). Our omitted category for income was the middle income group. We included the poor and rich race cohort interactions, and our omitted race category was white (see Table 4.1 for summary statistics).

Table 4.1. Summary statistics for U.S. data

Variable	Observations	*M*	*SD*	Min	Max
Gini index	468,032	0.459	0.0221	0.395	0.539
Log (median MSA household income)	468,032	10.92	0.179	10.41	11.42
Household income group	468,032	6.813	2.343	0	10
Poor household	468,032	0.194	0.395	0	1
Rich household	468,032	0.174	0.379	0	1
Age > 50	468,032	0.586	0.492	0	1
White	468,032	0.843	0.364	0	1
Black	468,032	0.0768	0.266	0	1
Hispanic	468,032	0.0219	0.146	0	1
Asian	468,032	0.0147	0.120	0	1
Other race	468,032	0.0437	0.204	0	1
(Poor household)*(white)	468,032	0.147	0.354	0	1
(Rich household)*(white)	468,032	0.154	0.361	0	1
(Poor household)*(black)	468,032	0.0251	0.156	0	1
(Rich household)*(black)	468,032	0.00766	0.0872	0	1
(Poor household)* (Hispanic)	468,032	0.00767	0.0872	0	1
(Rich household)* (Hispanic)	468,032	0.00199	0.0446	0	1
(Poor household)*(Asian)	468,032	0.00183	0.0428	0	1

Table 4.1. (*continued*)

Variable	Observations	M	SD	Min	Max
(Rich household)*(Asian)	468,032	0.00451	0.0670	0	1
(Poor household)* (other race)	468,032	0.0119	0.109	0	1
(Rich household)* (other race)	468,032	0.00619	0.0784	0	1
(White)*(age > 50)	468,032	0.521	0.500	0	1
(Black)*(age > 50)	468,032	0.0361	0.187	0	1
(Hispanic)*(age > 50)	468,032	0.00609	0.0778	0	1
(Asian)*(age > 50)	468,032	0.00428	0.0653	0	1
(Other race)*(age > 50)	468,032	0.0187	0.136	0	1
Age	468,032	52.85	16.33	18	99
Age-squared	468,032	3,060	1,751	324	9,801
Male	468,032	0.528	0.499	0	1
Married/cohabitating	468,032	0.599	0.490	0	1
Education level	468,032	4.149	1.503	1	6
BMI	468,032	27.41	5.591	9.486	106.8
Employed	468,032	0.631	0.483	0	1
Religious	468,032	0.630	0.483	0	1
Northeast	468,032	0.251	0.434	0	1
Midwest	468,032	0.214	0.410	0	1
South	468,032	0.306	0.461	0	1
West	468,032	0.229	0.420	0	1
Year 2008	468,032	0.413	0.492	0	1
Year 2009	468,032	0.327	0.469	0	1
Year 2010	468,032	0.260	0.439	0	1

In addition to individuals' household income, we included the log median income for each MSA, based on data from the American Community Survey, as well as year and region dummies. We explored the correlates of both present and future life satisfaction. In a subsequent specification, we added race-income-age interaction terms to explore the specific role of age in these beliefs channels. Because we are regressing individual-level variables on aggregate independent variables (MSA-level median income), we cluster our standard errors at the MSA level for all of our regressions.

Our baseline regression is:

Y_{it} *(BPL or BPLfut, for person i, in time period t)*
$$= \beta_0 + \beta_1 * (log\ median\ MSA\ level\ income) + \beta_2$$
* (poor household income group) + β_3 * (rich household income group)
+ β_4 * (black) + β_5 * (hispanic) + β_6 * (asian) + β_7
* (other race) + β_8 * (poor household income group) * (black) + β_9
* (poor household income group) * (hispanic) + β_{10}
* (poor household income group) * (asian) + β_{11}
* (poor household income group) * (other race) + β_{12}
* (rich household income group) * (black) + β_{13}
* (rich household income group) * (hispanic) + β_{14}
* (rich household income group) * (asian) + β_{15}
* (rich household income group) * (other race) + β_{16} * (age) + β_{17}
* (age^2) + β_{18} * (gender) + β_{19} * (education level) + β_{20}
* (health status as captured by BMI) + β_{21} * (employed) + β_{22}
* (religious, yes or no) + (region dummies) + (year dummies) + ε

where BPL and BPL future are, respectively, the dependent variables. The race variable is based on dummies for race categories, with whites as the omitted group.

We found that the usual correlates of life satisfaction held, as income, education, marriage, female gender, and religion were positively correlated, while health problem was negatively correlated. As is also usual, there is a U-shaped relationship between life satisfaction and age, turning in the mid-forties. The correlates of future life satisfaction displayed only modest differences. The coefficient on income became modestly weaker and that of education stronger, for example (Table A.4a).[3]

We get some interesting—and surprising—differences across both income and racial groups. On present life satisfaction, in addition to the usual

---

[3] We ran similar regressions with BPL and BPL future for the LAC region in the GWP poll and obtained very similar correlations across the main variables: age, income, gender, education, employment status, marital status, and so on. Regression results are available from the author.

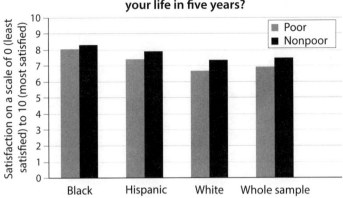

Figure 4.3a. Future life satisfaction across race and income cohorts.
Source: Author's calculations, based on Gallup Healthways data, 2008–2013.
Note: Average responses on a question that asks respondents to place themselves on a best possible life ladder five years into the future.

patterns, we find that Hispanics are modestly happier than whites, while blacks are modestly less happy and Asians much less happy. Yet our income and race interactions yield some different patterns. While rich blacks are less happy compared to rich whites, poor blacks are by far the happiest of all the poor * race groups. As such, there seems to be no additional premium (above and beyond the already positive overall effects of income) to being in the richest category and of a particular race. On future life satisfaction, the most striking finding is, again, the strong positive coefficient on poor blacks, who have much higher levels of optimism about future life satisfaction than any of the other poor * race cohorts (the difference is significantly larger than that for present life satisfaction). More generally, blacks and Hispanics in general are significantly more positive about their future happiness than are whites, while Asians are significantly less so. In separate specifications, meanwhile, we find that poor blacks also report less worry and stress than most other cohorts (discussed in detail below; see Figures 4.3a–4.3c).[4]

---

[4]Our positive coefficient on poor black is the most robust of all of our findings, and holds even when we create pseudo-panels for the full 2008–2014 sample and control for MSA fixed effects, which tend to reduce the significance of many other coefficients, but not those on the poor * black interaction term.

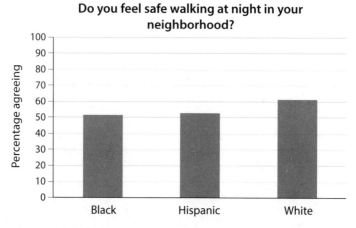

Figure 4.3b. Feeling safe across races and incomes.
Source: Author's calculations, based on Gallup Healthways data, 2008–2013.
Note: Average responses on a question that asks respondents (1) if they feel safe walking at night in their neighborhood and (2) whether religion is important in their lives. The scale for both questions is 0–1, with possible responses being no (0) or yes (1).

We next included our race and age interaction terms in our baseline regression in place of the race * income group interactions, again clustering our standard errors at the MSA level. Our equation is then:

Y_{it} (*BPL or BPLfut, for person i, in time period t*) $= \beta_0 + \beta_1$ * (*log median MSA level income*) $+ \beta_2$ * (*household group*) $+ \beta_3$ * (*age> 50*) $+ \beta_4$ * (*black*) $+ \beta_5$ * (*hispanic*) $+ \beta_6$ * (*asian*) $+ \beta_7$ * (*other race*) $+ \beta_8$*(*black*) *(*age > 50*) $+ \beta_9$ (*hispanic*) *(*age > 50*) $+ \beta_{10}$ * (*asian*) * (*age > 50*) $+ \beta_{11}$ * (*other race*) * (*age > 50*) $+ \beta_{12}$ * (*age*) $+ \beta_{13}$ *(*age²*) $+ \beta_{14}$ * (*gender*) $+ \beta_{15}$ * (*education level*) $+ \beta_{16}$ * (*health status as captured by BMI*) $+ \beta_{17}$ * (*employed*) $+ \beta_{18}$ * (*religious, yes or no*) $+$ (*region dummies*) $+$ (*year dummies*) $+ \varepsilon$

We find a strong positive coefficient on both life satisfaction and future life satisfaction for older blacks. It is the only significant positive age * race coefficient on present life satisfaction of all the groups. For future life satisfaction, older Asians also display a positive coefficient, but it is by no means as strong as that for older blacks (see Table A.4b). And, as in the case of poor

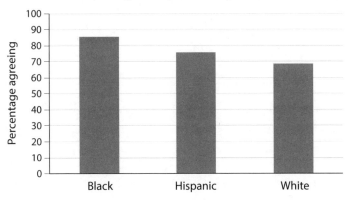

Figure 4.3c. Religion important across racial cohorts.
Source: Author's calculations, based on Gallup Healthways data, 2008–2013.
Note: Average responses on a question that asks respondents (1) if they feel safe walking at night in their neighborhood and (2) whether religion is important in their lives. The scale for both questions is 0–1, with possible responses being no (0) or yes (1).

blacks, older blacks also report lower levels of stress and worry than their counterpart cohorts of other races. Older blacks also report higher levels of social support than the average, followed by Hispanics (the regressions on stress and social support are presented and discussed in detail in the section on inequality below).

How significant are these findings in terms of order of magnitude? In terms of current life satisfaction, poor blacks have the strongest positive coefficient (by far) of any of the interaction terms, and the weight of that positive coefficient (0.546) by far outweighs the negative one (0.035) for blacks in general. As such, poor blacks score almost as high on current life satisfaction as middle-income whites. For future life satisfaction, the coefficient on poor blacks (0.401) is large enough to eliminate the difference between being poor (−0.482) and being middle class (e.g., removing the negative effect of poverty) on optimism about the future. And blacks in general are the most optimistic about the future of any group, which holds above and beyond the effects of the poor * black interaction term. As such, blacks—including poor blacks—score almost a full point (.7) higher on the future life satisfaction scale compared to middle-income whites, all else held equal.

A note of caution is necessary as selection bias is an issue. Both blacks and Hispanics are undersampled in the survey. The very poorest in bad straits may be less likely to answer Gallup surveys; in addition there is a high percentage of young black males who are incarcerated on the one hand, and a high percentage of poor Hispanics who are in the United States illegally (and therefore not likely to answer Gallup surveys) on the other.

What explains this surprising level of optimism among blacks and Hispanics in general, and among poor (and older) blacks in particular? It surely does not accord with the picture that comes from the recent riots in Baltimore and Ferguson, for example. Nor does it accord with much of what is written about the state of the social fabric in America.

Yet there are some plausible explanations. A recent article in the *Atlantic* noted remarkable optimism about the state of the country among blacks and Hispanics. In addition to being more optimistic about their future lives, blacks and Hispanics were also more optimistic about their personal station in life and about the future of the country more broadly (Berman, 2015). There also may an Obama effect, given the historical marker of the first African American president. Support for President Obama remained steady among blacks over the course of his tenure, for example, at the same time that it fell over time among many other cohorts.

A related issue is that over time, poor whites have fallen in status, as there is more competition for low-skilled jobs, such as from immigrants, while blacks in general have improved both their status and well-being, at least in relative terms. The overall black-white wage gap has narrowed (black males earned 69 percent of the median wage for white males in 1970 and 75 percent by 2013, most of the improvements were in the earlier decades; U.S. Census Bureau, 2014). Indeed, the largest increases in occupational aspirations and earnings of black men seem to have been in the years immediately following the civil rights movement, and then progress slowed after the economic downturn of the 1970s (Shu and Marini, 2008).

In contrast to the general stall in the trend toward more equal economic outcomes, while the gaps in achievement and proficiency have widened across income groups, in education they have narrowed between blacks (and Hispanics) and whites at the same time. Fifty years ago, the black-white proficiency gap was one and a half to two times as large as the gap between a child from a family at the top 90th percentile of the income distribution and a child from a family at the 10th percentile. Today the proficiency gap between the poor and the rich is nearly twice as large as that between black and white children (Porter, 2015).[5]

And gaps in health status and life expectancy between blacks and whites, while still significant, have also narrowed. The gap in life expectancy between whites and blacks was 7 years in 1990 (69.1 years for blacks versus 76.1 years for whites), while by 2014 it had narrowed to three years (75.6 versus 79.0 years). Homicide rates fell by 40 percent for blacks versus 28 percent for whites (albeit the former starting from a higher level) from 1995 to 2013, and the death rate from cancer during the same period fell by 29 percent for blacks versus 20 percent for whites (Tavernise, 2016).

As such, the differential beliefs in the future in part reflect actual changes in capacity to succeed in the future. And, likely related to this, the black-white happiness gap has also continued to narrow in the past years, likely because of improvements in civil rights and perceived status (Stevenson and Wolfers, 2013). Concurrently, while support for redistribution has remained the same among some cohorts in the United States, it has decreased over time among blacks. Support among blacks for assistance targeted to blacks in particular has fallen (Kuziemko et al., 2015).

Community and religious factors may also be at play. The riots in Baltimore and Ferguson had a clearly identified grievance—violence against blacks perpetrated by the police—and a deeper resentment against continued racism (Coates, 2015). Yet an equally if not more horrifying—but much more random—act of violence by a deranged white man in Charleston resulted not in black anger and violence, but in a tremendous show of community solidarity and support. While our regression analysis above includes controls for being religious in addition to the other variables, a simple visual look at the cross-tabulations on these scores is illustrative. While poor blacks are the most likely of all the poor groups to report that they are not safe walking in their neighborhoods at night, they are much more likely to report that religion is important in their lives, suggesting that religion may

---

[5] The 90/10 income achievement gap (in school readiness) grew by roughly 0.020 standard deviations per year among cohorts born in the mid-1970s to those born in the early 1990s. So the rate of decline in the kindergarten readiness 90/10 income gaps appears to be somewhere between 40 and 70 percent as rapid as the rate of increase in the gap in the prior two decades. See Reardon and Portilla (2015).

play an important role in helping them to deal with adversity (Figures 4.3b and 4.3c).

There also seem to be large differences in the experiences of poor, inner-city blacks compared to the rest of the black population. William Julius Wilson (2015) notes that while there is much attention to police crime against blacks, as in the case of Ferguson, an equally important and less known problem is the widening difference in the exposure to random violent crime that the poorest blacks in inner cities face compared to more affluent blacks and those who are not in inner cities. While the likelihood of being a victim of violent crime has fallen from roughly 40 percent to less than 20 percent in the past thirty years for more affluent blacks, it has increased from 40 percent to almost 70 percent for the poorest blacks in inner cities. The same social fabric that seems to be stronger in communities like Charleston is, no doubt, harder to sustain in the worst and most violent inner-city communities (and these communities are likely to be undersampled as well).

Some new work on aging, well-being, and race also sheds some light. James Jackson (2015), based on a long trajectory of work on minority well-being at the Institute for Social Research at Michigan, recently explored the "puzzle" of high subjective well-being among minorities in the National Survey of American Life. His framing theme is higher levels of resilience among certain populations, African Americans in particular, and he attributes this to adaptation, via adjusting expectations and cognitive beliefs. These findings echo some work by Ta-Nehisi Coates (2006, 2015), who explains black resilience in a more negative light, attributing it to resignation after decades of discrimination and unequal progress.

Indeed, there are many remaining obstacles to black progress. A major one is the continued housing segregation in many major American cities, such as Baltimore, Chicago, and Cleveland. Much of this is the result of discrimination in mortgage lending by major banks, a practice that was only recently addressed by public policy and regulation (Coates, 2006). The same cities that have higher rates of racial segregation also have much lower rates of social mobility (Chetty et al., 2014).

Jackson's findings on aging support the adaptation and adjusted expectations interpretation: younger blacks are, on average, much less happy than young whites, but then the patterns flip at roughly the middle age years, and then older blacks are happier than older whites. Indeed, African Americans are the happiest of all the elderly groups and are the least likely to display psychological distress.

Of the correlates of high levels of well-being later in life, Jackson finds that church attendance and emotional support from friends and family are the most important (and are typically higher among black respondents), with stronger coefficients than either health, years of schooling, and/or the poverty index. Another potential explanation that he raises is that "shedding" stressful roles, such as retiring from a stressful or low-quality job, is a good thing for well-being. Our data also show that poor blacks report less worry and stress than most other cohorts (reported below), and older blacks are more likely than others to report that they have friends and family whom they can rely on during times of need.

Jaqui Smith's (2015) work on the U.S. Health and Retirement Study supports these findings. She finds that while life satisfaction levels are higher, on average, for whites than for blacks, purpose in life is higher for blacks than whites, and frustration levels are lower. Finally Carol Ryff's (2015) recent work, based on the Mid-Life in the United States Study of eudemonic well-being, finds that minority status is a positive predictor of eudemonic well-being, and that blacks have a higher rate of "flourishing" than do whites. Ryff posits that the black-white gap would be even greater in the absence of discrimination. And, like other studies such as the one by Steptoe, Deaton, and Stone (2015), she finds that higher levels of eudemonic well-being are associated with lower mortality rates, a lower probability of Alzheimer's disease, and lower levels of perceived discrimination. The direction of causality is not clear in the latter case as those with higher levels of well-being are typically less likely to perceive discrimination, injustice, and/or inequality (for details on this issue, see Graham, 2009).

Some new research by psychiatrists Assari and Lankarani (2016) shows that while black Americans have worse health indicators than white Americans on average, they (and minority groups in general) are better off in terms of mental health. Depression, anxiety, and suicide are more common among whites than blacks, for example. The authors highlight higher levels of "resilience" among blacks and other minorities as an explanation. Resilience, which is defined as maintaining health in spite of a range of psychosocial risk factors, may be higher among blacks and minorities as they have had more experience with—and indeed a history of—dealing with adversity.

A complementary explanation and equally important part of the explanation is in the trends among poor whites, who, as noted above, are the least happy and optimistic group in the regression analysis. A recent study by Anne Case and Angus Deaton (2015) found that there was a marked increase in the all-cause mortality of high school (and below) educated white middle-aged non-Hispanic men and women between 1999 and 2013. The change reversed decades of progress in mortality and is unique to the United States and to non-Hispanic whites therein (Hispanic Americans have lower mortality rates, and the gap between blacks and whites, as noted above, has narrowed). The increasing mortality rate was driven by drug and alcohol poisoning, suicide, chronic liver diseases, and cirrhosis. Those respondents with the least education saw the greatest increases in these diseases. Self-reported health, mental health, and ability to conduct activities of daily living in this group also saw a marked decrease, and also suggest growing stress in this cohort.

What explains these stark trends among poor and near poor whites and in particular the contrast to the optimism (at least in relative terms) among poor blacks and Hispanics? Deaton (in Krugman, 2015) quotes anthropologist Caroline Rouse of Princeton University and notes that "middle aged whites are losing the narrative of their lives." Paul Krugman (2015) suggests, as do much of the data that I have presented throughout the chapter, that the economic setbacks of this group have been particularly bad because they expected better: "We're looking at people who were raised to believe in the American Dream, and are coping badly with its failure to come true." A recent study by Andrew Cherlin (2016) found that poor and middle-class blacks are more likely to compare themselves to parents who were worse off than they are when they are assessing their status. In contrast, poor and blue-collar whites, on average, have more precarious lives and employment stature than their parents did.

Raj Chetty and colleagues (2016), meanwhile, find that there are very strong geographic markers associated with these trends. Mortality rates and the associated behaviors are particularly prevalent in rural areas in the Midwest and much less so in cities. In part this is due to healthier behaviors associated with living in cities, such as more walking, and in part it is due to the combination of social isolation and economic stagnation that characterizes many of these rural locales. Krugman (2015) also notes the regional element to these trends: life expectancy is high and rising in the Northeast and California, where social benefits are highest and traditional values weakest, while low and stagnant life expectancy is concentrated in the Bible Belt (where economies are more stagnant as well). The most cited words in difficult places to live (described in Chapter 5)—guns, religion, hell, stress, diabetes, fad diets, and video games—are very relevant here.

In new research with Sergio Pinto (2016), I have started to match the CDC mortality rate data—using a composite variable that captures suicide, cirrhosis, drug overdose, and accidental deaths for forty-five- to fifty-four-year-olds—with our well (and ill) being metrics at the MSA level. We find that average levels of MSA future life satisfaction are negatively correlated with the mortality rate, while average levels of stress are positively correlated. We also find that MSAs that are more diverse (percentage of blacks and Hispanics) and those that have fewer respondents who smoke and more who exercise are more optimistic about the future and less stressed. These same places are more likely to be urban, reflecting the Chetty findings. While still preliminary, these findings suggest that well-being markers could serve as useful leading indicators.

Another potential way to think about the contrasts between the optimism of poor blacks and the pessimism of poor whites, which reflects their differential trends, is the loss aversion frame that Daniel Kahneman and Amos Tversky (1979) introduced to behavioral economics. He showed through numerous examples how individuals value losses disproportionately to gains. Poor whites are losing status, at least in relative terms, while poor blacks have begun to make significant gains, even though they have a long way to go to achieve parity on some levels, such as wages.

More generally, a more recent paper by Funke, Schularick, and Trebesch (2015), based on historical data, highlights the role of loss aversion in providing support for extremist (and particularly right-wing) politicians, which rises after financial crises in countries around the world. And that support is driven largely by cohorts who have experienced downward mobility and/or are threatened by it. In the 2016 elections in the United States it was those cohorts who either have experienced downward mobility or fear it who supported a candidate proposing to build walls, ban trade, and further divide society along racial and other lines.

In general, all of these studies highlight important differences across racial groups that may, in the longer run, help us understand hope and resilience in the face of poverty. Lack of hope and resilience among the most desperate ones, meanwhile, is a key feature of the tattered American Dream.

The Critical Roles of Stress and Income Inequality

Two important questions related to the above discussion about the high costs of poverty are (1) whether or not these attitudes matter to future behaviors and (2) to what extent they are related to the increasingly unequal distribution of income and opportunities in the United States. Our empirical work sheds light on these questions through two related explorations. The first focuses on whether the links between stress and markers of ill-being and short time horizons vary depending on levels of income and education. The second and related question is the role of inequality in the expectations, discount rates, beliefs, and behaviors channel. In the following empirical explorations, we again use data from the Gallup Daily and World Polls.

Good Stress, Bad Stress

Stress may vary as a "good" or "bad" influence depending on where in the income distribution respondents are. Stress that is related to daily struggles and an inability to plan ahead, as is typical for the poor and as cited in examples throughout the book, is both bad for well-being and a constraint on investing in the future. In contrast, stress that is related to hard work aimed at future benefit, such as going to graduate school, could have quite different and even positive effects.

My work with Ifcher and Zarghamee on inequality and well-being across U.S. MSAs and zip codes (discussed in Chapter 3) is suggestive of this "bad stress/good stress" distinction. We find that high levels of stress and other measures of negative hedonic well-being were associated with higher levels of average income (at both zip code and MSA levels). The main driving channel seems to be cost of living for those below median levels of income. At the same time, higher levels of stress are also associated with having individual incomes that are above the top income code and with being employed, both of which are also associated with higher levels of life satisfaction.

In this instance, in order to test this good and bad stress difference explicitly, Soumya Chattopadhyay and I ran separate regressions (as in earlier chapters, first with ordered logit specifications and then switching to OLS), with life satisfaction as the dependent variable and the usual sociodemographic and economic controls on the right-hand side. We also included reported stress and stress interacted with income, and began with the U.S. Gallup Healthways data.

$$Y_{it} \, (BPL \, for \, person \, i, \, in \, time \, period \, t) = \beta_0 + \beta_1 \text{ * } (socio-dem \, vector = age,$$
$$age^2, gender, marital \, status, BMI, education \, level) + \beta_2 \text{ * } (log \, income)$$
$$+ \beta_3 \text{ * } (stress) + \beta_4 \text{ * } (stress) \text{ * } (log \, income) + (year \, dummies) + \varepsilon$$

As in the earlier regressions in the book, life satisfaction is measured by the best possible life question in the Gallup Poll. Income in the Gallup Healthways is reported in ten brackets, with much smaller amounts of income in the bottom brackets (beginning with less than $30 per month) and the top bracket being above $10,000 per month. We took the log of the midpoint value in each bracket as the observation for each individual who reports to be in that respective bracket. We included the usual sociodemographic controls (age, age squared, gender, marital status, and education level) and then included BMI as a proxy for health status, as it was the one objective health indicator that was reported in all years. We also included year dummies.

The results provide support for the idea that stress has a different relation with well-being depending on individuals' means and capabilities (see Table A.5). Not surprisingly, the coefficient on stress demonstrates a significant and negative correlation with life satisfaction—with a value that is significantly greater (in negative terms) than the main correlates of life satisfaction, such as marital status and income. Our interaction term, however, is significant and positive, suggesting that at a certain level of income, the negative effects of stress are mitigated. We also found that higher levels of education mediated the negative effects of stress, although the coefficient was not as strong as that on income.

To estimate the order of magnitude of these effects, we first need to consider the effects of stress on life satisfaction independently, and then how those vary depending on how much income individual respondents have.

The negative effect of stress alone on life satisfaction, based on the coefficient in column 6, is −0.908, or roughly a decrease of almost an entire point on the ten-point life satisfaction scale. The mediating effect of income, meanwhile, which is logged, depends on what the respondent's starting income point is. For this calculation we use the coefficients in column 7, which includes the interaction between stress and income. The positive effects of log income on life satisfaction alone are 0.211, which in non-log terms translates to an increase of 1.46 on the ten-point scale. With stress (taking into account the interaction term of stress and income in addition to those on income alone and stress alone), holding all else constant, an individual with a monthly income of $1,000 who also reports to experience stress has an increase of 0.36 points.[6] Thus stress reduces the positive effect of income on life satisfaction by 1.1 points (1.46 − 0.36).

The mitigating effect of income on stress is more important at lower levels of income. For a respondent with a monthly income of $2,000 instead of $1,000, based on the same coefficients, magnitude of the positive income effect on life satisfaction is the 1.60 points on the ten-point scale. But the interaction term of income and stress results in a reduction of that positive effect of 0.61 points. Thus the mitigating effect is only 0.99 points on the life satisfaction scale (1.60 − 0.61) compared to 1.1 points for the individual with a monthly income of $1,000. Thus while those with more income typically have higher life satisfaction scores, income is relatively more important to mitigating stress for those with very low levels of income. It likely gives them some means to deal with stressful circumstances, and/or more control over those circumstances, while wealthier respondents already have such means.

As a comparison and robustness check, we ran the same regressions with Gallup World Poll data for Latin America as a whole. We find very similar results for LAC as we do for the United States: stress is negatively correlated with life satisfaction, but the interaction terms for both stress and income and stress and education, respectively, are positively correlated. As in the case of the United States, both income and education play a modest

---

[6] The calculation is thus: with stress, taking into account the interaction term of stress and income: 0.211 * log($1000) − 0.2099 (coefficient on stress in column 7) + 0.145 (coefficient on interaction term) * log($1000) = 0.036, holding all else constant, an individual with a monthly income of $2000 who also reports to experience stress has an increase of 0.36 points on the 0–10 scale, which is then subtracted from the 1.46-point effect of income without stress (= 1.1).

mitigating role on the negative effects of stress (for the regression results, see Table A.6).[7]

In sum, stress is, for the most part, negatively associated with well-being. Yet, as our findings suggest, stress that is associated with daily struggles and circumstances beyond individuals' control—as is more common for the poor—has more negative effects than that associated with goal achievement—as is more common for those with more means and education. In the case of the latter, the negative effects of stress are mediated by the positive effects of having enough means and education to invest in and plan for the future (and possibly also to cope with stress).

The studies cited and the data that we show throughout the book make it clear that the poor experience significantly higher levels of stress (and worry and anger and pain) than do the rich in the United States. The above results also suggest that the negative effects of that stress are worse for the well-being of the poor than they are for the rich, and that an additional increment of income does more (in relative terms) to reduce the negative effects of stress for the poor than for the rich.

A recent study by Sarah Fleche and Richard Layard (2015) on mental illness echoes the direction of these findings. In comparing trends in mental illness and misery (defined as being in the lowest part of the life satisfaction distribution) across Australia, Germany, the United Kingdom, and the United States, the authors find that mental illness has more explanatory power than poverty, unemployment, or physical health conditions in all four countries. Poverty—and the higher movements in and out of it—in the United States plays a relatively larger role than in the other countries. This is likely because of the higher levels of uncertainty (and stigma) associated with

---

[7] We also repeated the baseline good stress/bad stress regressions for Southeast Asia. Given that there were important differences in the means on stress, depending on whether or not China, Japan, and Korea were included in the whole sample, we ran the regressions first omitting China, Japan, and Korea; then with China only added in; and then with the full sample. For the first two specifications (Southeast Asia without China, Japan, and Korea, and then with China alone added in), we get findings that are very similar to those for the United States. Stress is negative and significant on life satisfaction, as expected, and there is a modest positive mitigating effect of both income and education. While in the United States the coefficient on the income term is stronger, in Asia that on education is stronger, perhaps because of the strong cultural focus on education in the latter. With Japan and Korea included, however, the coefficients on both income and education interaction terms are insignificant. It seems that the high levels of stress in these two countries wipe out any mitigating effects of higher levels of stress and education. In Japan and Korea, there seems to be just bad stress. Results are available from the author.

falling into poverty in the United States, as well as the associated desperation and stress that seem particularly marked for poor whites.

In what follows, we explore how stress varies (for both the poor and the rich and across races) according to local levels of inequality. We also explore how the role of social safety nets—which can help people cope with stress and insecurity—varies with stress.

The Mediating Role of Inequality: The Gatsby Curve in Attitudes

The Gatsby curve framework, established by Alan Krueger, Raj Chetty, and other authors (Krueger, 2012; Chetty et al., 2014) and discussed in Chapter 2, is a good way to begin thinking about inequality and its relation to potential beliefs and behaviors channels. That framework suggests that inequality in parental incomes (and other means) will result in even greater inequality for children, as their opportunities are increasingly linked to their parent's means. It is depicted visually and empirically in Figure 2.1, and shows a strong negative relationship between inequality in parental income (at the neighborhood or MSA level for 1996–2000) and the probability of a child born at the 25th percentile of the income distribution moving up the income ladder.

With this frame as a starting point, Sergio Pinto and I explored the relationship between inequality and markers of well-being and ill-being. We focused in particular on the incidence and distribution of two variables that reflect daily struggles and difficulty planning for and investing in the future: stress and worry. The above results suggest not only that the poor experience more stress than the rich in the United States, but that the negative effects of stress are worse for the poor. The stress of the poor is associated with circumstances that are beyond their control, making it more difficult for them to plan ahead and invest in their futures. In contrast, the stress experienced by the rich is typically associated with goal achievement and investments in education. As such, the gaps between the poor and the rich (and their children) are likely to grow greater, as in the Gatsby hypothesis.

We used MSA-level income inequality, as measured by the Gini coefficient (as well as alternative measures of inequality, such as the 90/10 ratio, as robustness checks), on the horizontal axis and the average incidence of stress and worry, respectively, on the vertical axis. The inequality data came from the 2013 the American Community Survey (ACS). And, as a reminder, the Gini coefficient runs from 0 to 1, where zero represents a completely equal distribution of income in a society and 1 represents a society where only one individual holds all the wealth. We repeated the same exercise but with the distribution of stress and worry across the rich and poor on the vertical axis. Figures 4.4a and 4.4b show the results. (For a distribution of inequality across MSAs, see Figure A.2.)[8]

We find that the average incidence of stress and worry is higher in more unequal MSAs. We also find that the distribution of these variables is more unequal in more unequal MSAs: the rich-poor differentials in both stress and worry are greater in MSAs with higher Gini coefficients. Finally, the graphs also suggest a higher concentration of both stress and worry among the poor in more unequal MSAs, while values for the rich are essentially flat across the MSAs.[9]

A key mechanism for coping with stresses and struggles in many contexts, meanwhile, is friends, family, and other social networks that people can rely on in times of need. These networks serve as a particularly important safety net for those for whom formal mechanisms (ranging from stable jobs to health insurance) are weak (Graham, 1994). Social networks tend to be stronger in more cohesive societies, and can also be undermined by visible manifestations of inequality, as the above-cited work by Nishi and colleagues (2015) suggest.

Using the same framework as that for stress and worry, we explored whether beliefs about having a social network one could rely on varied by MSA-level inequality. We used a question in the Gallup Healthways that asks respondents if they have friends or family they can rely on in times of trouble (with possible answers being yes or no). We found that the percentage of respondents reporting yes—e.g., average level of beliefs that such safety nets

---

[8] The most equal MSAs, with Ginis at .39, were Fond du Lac, Wisconsin, and Ogden-Clearfield, Utah. The most unequal MSAs, with Ginis over .50 were the Bridgeport, Connecticut, area; New York–Newark–Jersey City; Naples–Immobalee–Marco Island, Florida; and Sebastien–Vero Beach, Florida.

[9] As a robustness check we repeated our analysis for MSAs with over a hundred household observations for both rich and poor households, as some of the MSAs in the full sample had fewer than that. The absolute incidence of stress and worry for both rich and poor holds for more unequal MSAs, but the gap between them loses statistical significance in this specification.

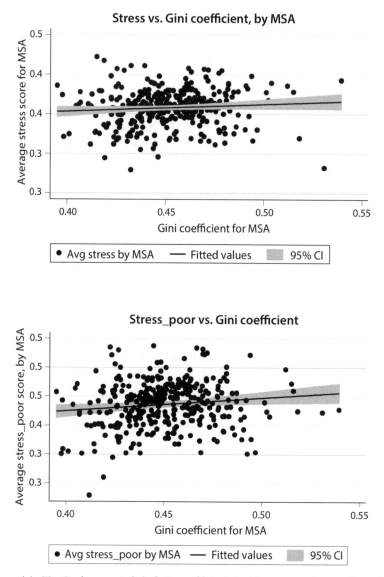

Figure 4.4a. The Gatsby curve in beliefs: Stress. (i) Stress incidence versus Gini coefficient by MSA. (ii) Stress incidence among poor versus Gini coefficient by MSA.
Source: Gallup Daily Poll 2008–2013; 2009–2013, 5-Year American Community Survey.

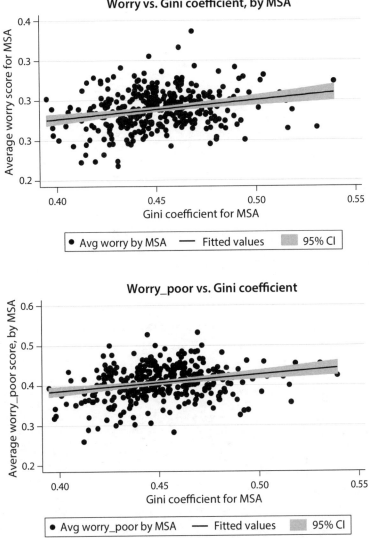

Figure 4.4b. The Gatsby curve in beliefs: Worry. (i) Worry incidence versus Gini coefficient by MSA. (ii) Worry incidence among poor versus Gini coefficient by MSA.
Source: Gallup Daily Poll 2008–2013; 2009–2013, 5-Year American Community Survey.

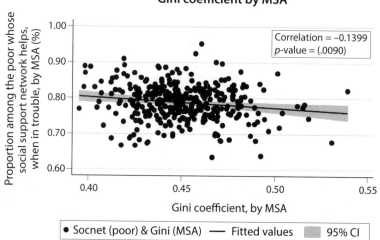

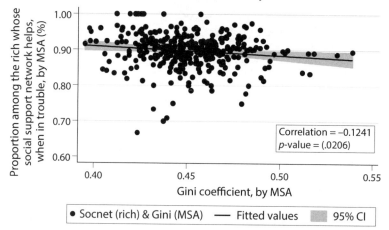

Figure 4.4c. The Gatsby curve in beliefs: Social network support. (i) Social support network among poor versus Gini coefficient by MSA. (ii) Social support network among rich versus Gini coefficient by MSA.

Source: Gallup Daily Poll 2008–2013; 2009–2013, 5-Year American Community Survey.

Stress incidence vs. Gini coefficient by MSA

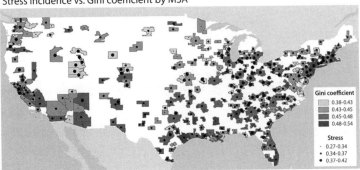

Worry incidence vs. Gini coefficient by MSA

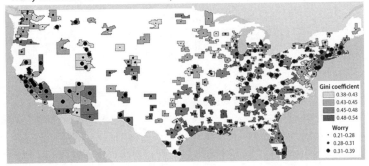

Figure 4.4d. Maps of stress incidence and worry incidence versus Gini coefficient by MSA. *Source*: Gallup Daily Poll 2008–2013; 2009–2013, 5-Year American Community Survey.

existed—was inversely correlated with MSA-level inequality. We also found that both the rich and the poor were less likely to report that they had such social support in more unequal MSAs, suggesting that there is less social cohesion (or belief in such cohesion) in more unequal MSAs. (The correlation coefficient was slightly more negative for the poor, −.14, than for the rich, −.12). Thus in more equal MSAs virtuous cycles—less stress and worry, more social support—reinforce each other, while in less equal ones, more stress and worry coexist with less social support (see Figure 4.4c; for maps of local inequality and stress and worry, see Figure 4.4d).

We explored whether respondents' satisfaction with place also varied by inequality levels, based on a question in Gallup that asks respondents if they are satisfied or dissatisfied with the city in which they live. Not surprisingly

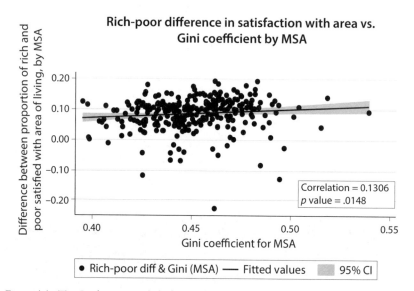

Figure 4.4e. The Gatsby curve in beliefs: Satisfaction with city.
Source: Gallup Daily Poll 2008–2013; 2009–2013, 5-Year American Community Survey.
Note: The rich-poor difference is obtained by subtracting, in each MSA, the difference in proportion of satisfied among the poor from the proportion among the rich. Increasingly positive values and an upward slope indicate a widening disparity between rich and poor.

given the above findings, we found that the rich-poor ratio in levels of satisfaction with city increases along with inequality, and that difference is largely driven by the poor, who are less satisfied in more unequal cities, while the curve for the rich is flat (see Figure 4.4e).

We also looked at an additional variable—"Were you treated with respect yesterday?"—and found that it was positively correlated with the MSA-level Gini coefficients. When we broke it down, we found that the positive correlation was for the rich, but was not significant for the poor; in other words the rich were more likely to feel that they were treated with respect in places with higher levels of inequality but the poor were not.[10]

A note of caution is necessary. Correlation is not causation, and there are unobservable differences across MSAs that could also be correlated with more stress, weaker social contracts, and lower levels of satisfaction than

[10]Results are available from the author.

place, and could also be part and parcel of higher levels of inequality. While we cannot prove whether it is inequality per se—or unobservable features of it—driving our findings, they highlight a clear negative association with well-being. In addition (although less of a concern), it is possible that the small number of observations in some of the MSAs introduces some bias. Yet our results held when we kept only the MSAs with over one hundred observations for each of the poor and rich subgroups.

To introduce more precision and address these concerns to the extent that we could, we explored the association between MSA-level inequality and individual-level life satisfaction, stress, worry, and social support in a multivariate regression framework. In three similar specifications, but with each of the well-being questions (respectively) as the dependent variables, we included the same independent variables as in the regressions on future life satisfaction above: age, gender, marital status, household income group, race, BMI (as a proxy for health status), employment status, and religious (or not). We also (again) included interaction terms for race * income level, log of MSA median income (also from the ACS), MSA Gini coefficients, and region and year dummies.

Because we have only one Gini observation per MSA, we could not also include MSA-level dummies due to multicollinearity. As such and as noted above, there are surely unobservable characteristics specific to particular MSAs that we are not able to control for. As an attempt to correct for this, we cluster the standard errors at the MSA level for all of the regressions.

Our equations are thus:

$$
\begin{aligned}
WB_{it} = {} & \beta_0 + \beta_1 * (MSA\ Gini\ coefficient) + \beta_2 * (log\ median\ MSA \\
& level\ income) + \beta_3 * (poor\ household\ income\ group) + \beta_4 \\
& * (rich\ household\ income\ group) + \beta_5 * (black) + \beta_6 * (hispanic) \\
& + \beta_7 * (asian) + \beta_8 * (other\ race) + \beta_9 * (poor\ household\ income\ group) \\
& * (black) + \beta_{10} * (poor\ household\ income\ group) * (hispanic) + \beta_{11} \\
& * (poor\ household\ income\ group) * (asian) + \beta_{12} * (poor\ household\ income \\
& group) * (other\ race) + \beta_{13} * (rich\ household\ income\ group) * (black) \\
& + \beta_{14} * (rich\ household\ income\ group) * (hispanic) + \beta_{15} * (rich\ household \\
& income\ group) * (asian) + \beta_{16} * (rich\ household\ income\ group) * (other \\
& race) + \beta_{17} * (age) + \beta_{18} * (age^2) + \beta_{19} * (gender) + \beta_{20} * (education
\end{aligned}
$$

$$level) + \beta_{21} * (health\ status\ as\ captured\ by\ BMI) + \beta_{22} * (employed)$$
$$+ \beta_{23} * (religious,\ yes\ or\ no) + (region\ dummies) + (year\ dummies) + \varepsilon$$

where WB_{it} is the particular well-being variable (life satisfaction, stress, worry, and social support respectively) for individual i at time t. As is standard in the literature, we use OLS regressions for the ten-point scaled life satisfaction question, and logit regressions for the other three variables, which are all dichotomous yes/no questions. The omitted dummy for income is "middle-class household" and for race is "white" for all regressions in Tables A.7a and A.7b.

Our findings are remarkably consistent and indeed more robust than the simple correlations of average levels and MSA-level Ginis above. We find that life satisfaction (based on the usual BPL question) is negatively correlated both with being in a higher Gini MSA and with MSA-level median income, while the usual variables that correlated positively with life satisfaction, such as marital status, income, education, and employment, run in the expected direction. High levels of BMI are usually a marker of ill health and thus not surprisingly are negatively correlated with life satisfaction.

Our race and income interactions in the specification with inequality included demonstrate similar trends as they do in the above section. While blacks, Hispanics, and whites all have higher life satisfaction levels than either Asians or "other" races, the negative interaction term of rich blacks and rich Hispanics roughly offsets the positive coefficients on black and Hispanics. In other words, while blacks and Hispanics in general display above average life satisfaction scores, rich blacks and Hispanics do not display levels that are any higher. In contrast, the interaction terms for poor and race again show that poor blacks and poor Hispanics have much higher levels of life satisfaction than the average, while poor whites are much lower than the average (Table A7a).

The stress and worry results operate in a similar but mirror fashion. Both stress and worry levels are higher in higher inequality MSAs, while the socioeconomic and demographic correlates of stress and worry are the inverse of those for life satisfaction. And while blacks and Hispanics in general have lower stress and worry levels than whites, rich blacks and Hispanics are no different from rich whites on stress and worry levels. Poor blacks and poor Hispanics have lower levels of stress and worry than poor whites, meanwhile, which is not surprising given the findings on life satisfaction and future life satisfaction discussed above. In terms of orders of magnitude, poor whites are 57 percent more likely to experience stress in the previous day, relative to middle-class whites, while middle-class Blacks are 36 percent less likely to experience stress relative to middle-class whites. And while poor blacks are 44 percent more likely to experience stress in the previous day than middle-class blacks, that differential is less than that between poor and middle-class whites.[11]

Our social support variable also demonstrates a clear negative correlation with MSA-level inequality, supporting the graphs above and that the relationship holds across income groups. In general, wealthy households report more social support than poor ones. Yet the findings on race differ from those on life satisfaction, stress, and worry. Indeed, despite the very positive scores of poor blacks on the other well-being variables above, they show no significant differences on social support than poor whites or poor Hispanics. Blacks and Hispanics in general show lower levels of support than whites (see Table A.7a). One difference, though, that is worthy of note is that when we explored age * race rather than income * race categories, we found that elderly blacks (e.g., over age fifty) report higher levels of social support than other older cohorts, followed by older Hispanics (see Table A.7b).

Overall, we find a clear negative association between MSA-level inequality and well-being, to the extent that our Gini coefficient variable is capturing inequality per se. While there are clearly unobservable traits within in MSA's that we are unable to control for in our regressions, it is unlikely that these traits are the same in all high (or low) Gini MSA's, as they are located in distinct and very different locations, among other things. And the fact that the relationship holds across different well-being dimensions (as well as for

---

[11] The coefficients on stress are as follows: Stress = B0 + B1 * Poor (0.451) + B2 * Black (−0.453) + B3 * Poor * Black (−0.086). The interpretation would be as follows, which requires transforming log income into linear income: $e^{B1} = e^{(0.451)} = 1.57$. For poor whites, the odds of experiencing stress in the previous day are 1.57 times those of middle-class whites, holding all else held equal. For middle-class blacks (B2) the interpretation would be as follows: $e^{B2} = e^{(−0.453)} = 0.636$. The odds of experiencing stress in the previous day for middle-class blacks are 0.636 times those of middle-class whites, holding all else fixed. While interpreting the interaction term is more complex, a plausible one is based on: $e^{(B1 + B3)} = e^{(0.451 − 0.086)} = 1.44$. As such, the odds of experiencing stress in the previous day for poor blacks are 1.44 times those of middle-class blacks, holding all else held equal.

social support and respect as reported above) suggests a consistent pattern, even if we cannot fully explain what it is.

A simple example provides a sense of the order of magnitude of the effect of MSA-level inequality on well-being. Imagine changing from an MSA with a Gini of 0.42 to one of 0.43, a 0.01 increase. This is analogous to moving from Fort Knox, Kentucky, to Green Bay, Wisconsin. Based on the negative coefficients on the MSA-level Ginis, this would imply a difference in life satisfaction across those MSAs of 0.01120 on the ten-point scale. While this does not seem like a large numerical effect, given that Ginis vary by very little and that the reduction applies to average life satisfaction across an entire MSA in addition to the effects of all other confounding factors that we control for, it is still notable.

The differences between the most equal and unequal MSAs in the country are much larger, meanwhile. The most equal MSAs in the United States are Fond du Lac, Wisconsin, and Ogden-Clearfield, Utah, each with a Gini of 0.39, and the most unequal MSA is the Bridgeport, Connecticut, area, with a Gini of 0.5391. Thus instead of a 0.01 difference as in our first example, the difference of 0.14 is more than ten times as large between these MSAs, and the resulting life satisfaction difference would also be more than ten times as large.

The stress, worry, and social support variables are binary and thus are interpreted a bit differently than is the life satisfaction variable (which behaves like a continuous variable in the regressions).[12] Using the same example of moving up one Gini point (from 0.42 to 0.43 again) and based on the coefficients on stress, worry, and social support, the odds that an individual in the higher inequality MSA experiences stress are 1.0191 times those of an individual living in the less unequal one. The same figures for worry and social support are 1.0328 and 0.9817, respectively. In percentage terms, an individual in an MSA with Gini that is 0.01 higher would have a 2 percent increase in the odds of experiencing stress, a 3 percent increase in the odds

---

[12] Logit models calculate the probability that an individual will be in one category or the other (yes or no) in terms of log odds. As such, it is necessary to use the exponential value of the coefficients in calculating the probabilities above. As an example, based on the coefficient on stress, where the coefficient we obtain on the Gini is 1.892, and we use a change in the Gini of 0.1, the change in odds of experiencing stress = e^(1.892 * 0.1) = e^(0.1892) = 1.208. If the change in the Gini were of 0.01 instead, we would have: the change in odds of experiencing stress = e^(1.892 * 0.01) = e^(0.01892) = 1.019.

of experiencing worry, and a 1 percent decrease in the odds of having social support than would an individual in an MSA that is 0.1 points lower (e.g., comparing respondents in Fort Knox and Green Bay).

A larger 0.1-point difference in the Gini coefficients between the MSAs (slightly less than the difference between Fond du Lac and Bridgeport) would bring the changes in the odds to 1.38, 1.21, 0.83, respectively. In this latter case, we can expect an increase in the odds of experiencing worry of 38 percent and in experiencing stress of 21 percent, and a decrease in the odds of having social support of 17 percent.

The findings on our race categories, meanwhile, link back to those earlier in this chapter about expectations about the future, and find remarkably positive trends in well-being for poor blacks and Hispanics and worrisome ones for their poor white counterparts. And, again, we find evidence of lower well-being levels among wealthy minorities. While we cannot explain the latter finding, it may be a result of either raised expectations or, alternatively, frustrated expectations after certain benchmarks, such as higher income levels, have been met.

Our Gatsby curves in beliefs thus highlight lower well-being as measured by life satisfaction, stress, and worry, and also as support mechanisms to cope with stress and other challenges, in more unequal places. To the extent that the stress experienced by the poor is largely driven by daily struggles and a related inability to plan for and invest in the future, and the stress experienced by the rich is associated with goal achievement such as in education, then the differences between the poor and the rich—and their children—will only grow larger, as in the Gatsby hypothesis.

Weak social networks and safety nets in more unequal places represent yet another channel that can perpetuate and increase these differences. In contrast, in related work, Tuugi Chuluun and I find that MSAs with higher levels of average MSA-level life satisfaction—and less inequality in life satisfaction (as measured by the standard deviation in life satisfaction scores)—are associated with more firm investment and more vibrant economic climates in general (Chuluun and Graham, 2016).

As in the example of Peru at the beginning of the chapter, there are often additional high costs to being poor, which are passed on from parents to children. While in Peru in the 1970s the costs of lack of access to basic services were passed on via children's health outcomes, in the United States today the costs of low expectations, high levels of stress and worry, and lack of social support are likely to exhibit themselves across a range of children's outcomes.

A Story of Two Americas

There are many markers of the high costs of being poor in the land of the American Dream. The objective ones are well known and have been documented extensively elsewhere. They are fewer markers of material deprivation and more markers of inability to take up opportunities and to exit poverty, such as poor educational attainment, low wages, unstable jobs, fractured families, and dysfunctional neighborhoods. And all of these combine to make it difficult for children born into families with these markers to exit out of poverty.

The beliefs and behaviors channels that stem from and perpetuate the prohibitive costs of poverty are less well known but equally important. High levels of stress related to uncertainty and daily struggles and low expectations for the future due to a range of factors—from childhood experience of discrimination to the distance between the poor and their "successful" wealthy and educated counterparts in society—can result in short-term time horizons and fewer investments in the future. The following chapter will provide numerous examples of studies—from a range of disciplines—that identify linkages between these short-term time horizons and the behaviors and outcomes of the poor.

In the aggregate, the empirical findings in this chapter confirm the increasingly consistent story of "two Americas," with the poor much less likely to be optimistic about their futures than the rich. Along with increasing levels of inequality and stagnation in mobility rates have come increasing divisions among the rich and the poor in the United States, divisions in terms of means, capabilities, and ability to plan for the future; opportunities and outcomes; well-being and markers of ill-being; and hope, aspirations for the future, and faith in the American Dream. Equally notable, though, are very high levels of optimism among poor blacks relative to poor whites, and slightly lower but still notable optimism levels among poor Hispanics. Traditionally marginalized groups are making gradual gains in narrowing the gaps with whites and are also more likely to be optimistic about their futures.

Poor and near poor whites have realistic fears of falling further behind and are showing signs of desperation.

We explored the stress associated with short time horizons as a factor in the negative beliefs and behaviors channel. Our findings suggest that there is good stress and bad stress, with opportunities and capabilities being a key mediating factor. The negative well-being effects of stress are mitigated for the rich due to its association with goal achievement and investments in a better future life. They are worse for the poor as stress is associated with daily struggles and circumstances beyond individuals' control, and contributes to their inability to plan for the future.

Income inequality, meanwhile, has a role in this story. Our findings on MSA-level inequality and important markers of well-being (and ill-being) highlight inequities that have implications for future generations—a Gatsby curve in well-being of sorts. We find a greater incidence of stress and worry in general in more unequal MSAs (at both the aggregate and individual levels), and also greater rich-poor differences in the distribution of these variables, with the association, not surprisingly, stronger for the poor. We also find that higher inequality is associated with lower levels of life satisfaction, which in part reflects capacity to have hopes for and to make choices about the future (although there are again large differences between poor blacks and Hispanics on the one hand, and poor whites on the other).

We also find that the mechanisms that can help individuals cope with stress and daily struggles—networks of family and friends—are weaker in more unequal places, providing an additional channel by which those suffering stress and daily struggles can fall further and further behind those who have much greater means to cope and to invest in their futures. Our findings suggest that the Gatsby curve in opportunities has an additional beliefs and behaviors channel that may perpetuate and deepen inequality over time.

The following chapter reviews a nascent but growing literature on this beliefs and behaviors channel. While much is very new research, it is suggestive of a strong link between low expectations and inferior future outcomes, which, in turn, makes our findings on inequality of hope and expectations for the future in the United States even more worrisome (see Figure A.2 and Table 4.1).

CHAPTER 5

Well-Being, Aspirations, and Outcomes

What Do We Know?

"Would you tell me please, which way I ought to go from here?" asked Alice. "That depends a good deal on where you want to get to," said the Cat. "I don't much care where," said Alice. "Then it doesn't matter which way you go," said the Cat.

—*Lewis Carroll,* Alice's Adventures in Wonderland[1]

This quote highlights the link between prospects for the future and the willingness and capacity to invest in it. As Alice does not really care where she goes, there is no clear path to a better fate. A more recent—and real-world—example of this same phenomenon comes from David Leonhardt (2015) and his colleagues at the New York Times. Their study was based on a Google search of the most common words used by those who live in the most difficult places in America and then those who live in the easiest places (for example Detroit and Baltimore versus Seattle and Portland).

The common words in "poor America" were obesity, diabetes, stress, fad diets, guns, video games, hell, and anti-Christ. These words reflect the extent to which many poor Americans juggle health problems and other daily struggles with patchwork solutions that reflect their inability to control—and or perhaps even care about—their own destinies, like Alice. The words most commonly used in the easy places to live were iPads, BabyBjörn, foam rollers, baby joggers, and exotic travel destinations such as Machu Picchu. The words

---

[1] I thank Daphna Oyserman for highlighting this quotation for me.

of "rich America" reflect investments in knowledge, health, exercise, and the next generation. It is not difficult to imagine how different the futures of each cohort will be.

In the previous chapters I used surveys of well-being to highlight the extent to which the rich and the poor in the United States have very different visions of the future, and explored the role of income, income inequality, and stress, among other factors, in explaining those differences. Despite the very large differences between rich and poor, meanwhile, I also found equally important ones across poor cohorts, with poor whites being the least optimistic group by far, while poor blacks were the most optimistic.

In this chapter, I explore the channels via which the differences in outlooks for the future that I find are likely to lead to very different outcomes within and across generations. A modest but growing body of research finds that higher levels of evaluative well-being lead to investments in the future and in better future outcomes, as in the labor market and health arenas. I review that literature with a particular focus on the linkages between well-being (in its distinct dimensions), positive attitudes about the future, and behavioral outcomes in the health, income, and social arenas.

These linkages are not simple to establish and prove empirically. We lack sufficient data following the same people over time, which would allow us to compare their attitudes at an initial point in time with their outcomes later on, holding all other factors constant. In addition, the causal channels entail a mix of objective circumstances that determine future outlooks on the one hand and unobservable personality traits on the other, making it difficult to clearly establish the direction of causality. Despite these difficulties, the growing body of literature confirms the existence of a beliefs and behaviors channel that operates in a wide range of settings (well beyond the United States). The most recent research in this area attempts to explore the causal channels to the extent possible, and requires approaches that cross a wide range of disciplines, from economics, sociology, and psychology on the one hand to the medical sciences on the other.

Some of my very early work in this area, coauthored with Andy Eggers and Sandip Sukhtankar (2004), based on panel data for Russia, showed that higher levels of "residual" happiness—e.g., the happiness of each individual that was not explained by observable socioeconomic and demographic traits—in an initial period regression (in t-0) was correlated with higher levels of income and better health in later periods. The effects were greater for individuals at lower levels of income. And, indeed, one can imagine that for workers with less income and education to leverage, a positive attitude or cheery character may well have payoffs in the labor market. The work by Shanahan and colleagues (2014) on the United States, discussed in Chapter 3, highlights how positive personality traits are more important to the attainment of low SES kids because they play a substitution role in the case of lower investments in human capital. Diener, King, and Lyubormirsky (2005), meanwhile, review a number of psychological studies, including their own, and find that individuals with higher levels of cheerfulness and positive affect did better in later life, in both the income and friendship realms.

The research has developed in more recent years. De Neve and Oswald (2012) used a large U.S. representative panel to show that young adults who report higher life satisfaction or positive affect grew up to earn significantly higher levels of income later in life. They used twins and siblings as comparison controls and accounted for factors such as intelligence and health, as well as the human capacity to imagine later socioeconomic outcomes and anticipate the resulting feelings in current well-being. Ifcher and Zarghamee (2011), based on experimental data, isolate the effects of mild positive affect in reducing time preferences over money and in the ability to delay gratification. Oswald, Proto, and Sgroi (2015), also based on experimental data, showed that positive affect induced by video clips resulted in subjects putting forth a greater quantity of output (10–12 percent), although with no difference in quality. They also found that bad moods induced by bereavement or illness in the subjects' families had a negative effect on productivity.

De Neve and coauthors (2013) conducted a general review of the existing research on well-being and positive outcomes. They found that there were benefits in the health arena, such as improved cardiovascular health, boosted immune and endocrine systems, lowered risk of heart disease, stroke, and infection, healthier behaviors, speedier recovery, and increased survival rates and longevity. In the income and social arenas the studies found increased productivity; higher peer-rated and financial performance; reduced absenteeism; greater creativity, cognitive flexibility, cooperation, and collaboration; higher income; greater organizational performance; reduced consumption and increased savings; boosted employment; reduced risk taking; greater prosocial behavior (altruism, volunteering), sociability, social relationships, and networks; and, critical to the focus of this chapter, longer-term time preferences and delayed gratification.

Studies that specifically focus on the links between life satisfaction and health find effects that include reduced inflammation, better cardiovascular health and immune systems, and healthier behaviors, among others (Blanchflower, Oswald, and Stewart-Brown, 2012; Davidson, Mostofsky, and Whang, 2010; Kubzansky, Gilthorpe, and Goodman, 2012). Of course it could be that healthier people are happier and not the other way around, or that causality runs in both directions (Graham, 2008). Some studies have been able to isolate the linkage from happiness to health, such as optimism predicting future outcomes such as immune function and cancer outcomes, controlling for health and demographic factors, and optimism and positive emotions protecting against cardiovascular disease (Rasmussen, Scheier, and Greenhouse, 2009; Boehm and Kubzansky, 2012).

The same studies identify stress as a factor that can hinder healing after injury. Stress continually appears as a negative analogue to the positive well-being–outcomes link, and instead reflects difficulty getting beyond daily struggles, short time horizons, and worse health, among other things. Its negative role, particularly for the poor, was highlighted in the empirical results in Chapter 4.

A very recent study by Liu et al. (2015), meanwhile, focuses specifically on unhappiness and mortality rates and finds no direct causal relationship. The authors use over-time data on British women and control for self-rated health, treatment for hypertension, diabetes, asthma, arthritis, depression, and anxiety, and a range of sociodemographic and lifestyle factors (such as BMI and exercise). They find that self-reported health has a very strong relation with mortality rates, but that unhappiness is insignificant. They note that unhappiness may be associated with many of the behaviors that heighten mortality risk, and at the same time that ill health may cause unhappiness, but do not find a direct link between unhappiness and mortality above and beyond all of these other controls.

Indeed, their findings are not surprising given the associated factors that they control for, such as depression/anxiety and low levels of health satisfaction, which are associated with both unhappiness and mortality. As such it is difficult to imagine that an additional measure of unhappiness would have any weight at all.

It is also important to note that in all of the literature cited above, most studies do not suggest that happiness alone can cure fatal diseases such as cancer, but instead that the associated positive character traits and biological markers of well-being seem to play a positive and significant role in the process of healthy living and the challenges of chronic disease as people age. Still, the finding that unhappiness is associated with the kinds of behaviors that limit life spans complements those above that highlight the positive channels between happiness, better health, and longevity.[2]

There are also linkages between well-being and individual and social behaviors, as De Neve et al. (2013) note in their review. Positive affect seems to be linked to lower discount rates in terms of consumption, and happy individuals seem to be motivated to pursue long-term goals despite short-term costs. In contrast, lack of self-control is related to overconsumption and unhappiness, as in the case of excessive television watching, cigarette smoking, and obesity (Frey, Benesch, and Stutzer, 2007; Gruber and Mullainathan, 2005; Graham, 2008). Greater self-control and longer-term time preferences among happier people have also been linked to consumption and savings behaviors. Based on longitudinal household data from Germany and the Netherlands, Guven (2012) finds that happier people are more likely to consume less and save more than others, and also have higher perceived life expectancies. Goudie et al. (2014) find that individuals with higher levels of subjective well-being are more likely to wear seatbelts and less likely to be in motor vehicle accidents, highlighting longer time preferences and less risk taking.

It is worth noting the growing gap in life expectancy between rich and poor in the United States, given this context and the broader focus on differential discount rates. While an average man in the upper income bracket was expected to live to age eighty-nine, and the average woman in that bracket to age ninety-two, the average man/woman in the lower income brackets was expected to live to seventy-six and seventy-eight years, respectively. Differential behaviors explain some of this, meanwhile. The poor are much more likely to be obese and to smoke cigarettes than are the rich, for example (Ehrenfreund, 2015; National Academy of Sciences, 2015). Yet those behaviors explain only a third of the gap; the rest can be attributed to a range of factors, from stress (which, as noted above, makes it more difficult for individuals to have long-term time horizons), early childhood health, and even prenatal

---

[2] An additional technical concern is that the happiness question came immediately after the health satisfaction question in their questionnaire, likely biasing responses and linking them more closely than they might otherwise have been.

differences. In addition, the latest mortality data, highlighted in Case and Deaton (2015), suggest an important role for suicide, drug and opioid addiction, and other self-inflicted or desperation-related causes of death among these cohorts.

As noted above, there is a related and relatively new emphasis in economics on noncognitive skills in determining economic choices and behaviors. Measures of these skills include personality traits such as conscientiousness, extraversion, openness to experience, and emotional stability; creativity; and self-esteem. Echoing many above-cited works, findings of research in this area show these skills to be important predictors of educational and labor market outcomes, such as completing higher levels of education, productivity, retention rates, and wage levels (see, for example, Heckman, Stixrud, and Urzua, 2006, and Bowles, Gintis, and Osborne, 2001).

Heidi Buddelmeyer and Nick Powdthavee (2015) build from this, as well as the work of many psychologists such as George Bonanno (2005) on resilience and related traits, and look at the specific properties of locus of control. They define locus of control as a person's belief or expectancy regarding the nature of the causal relationship between his or her behavior and its consequences. Internal locus of control is the belief that much of what happens in life stems from one's own actions, while external locus of control is the belief that events in life are primarily outcomes of factors such as fate, luck, and other people.

People who have an internal locus of control tend to invest more in human capital accumulation because their expected return to human capital investment is higher (see Cobb-Clark, 2015). They also tend to live a healthier lifestyle through better diets and more exercise, save more for the future, and invest more time in stimulating their children intellectually. In short, those who believe in their future—and also that they have some control over it—are much more likely to invest in those futures than those who do not, a finding related to much of the other work reviewed in this book.

Buddelmeyer and Powdthavee use the Australian HILDA panel to test whether internal locus of control (as gauged by a question in the survey about whether or not individuals believe that their actions can influence future outcomes) helps individuals navigate negative shocks. They find that respondents with higher levels of internal locus of control also have some insurance from negative shocks. They recuperate more quickly psychologically from their own and others' serious illness or injury, having a close family member detained in jail, becoming a victim of property crime, and the death of a close friend. And, as noted in earlier chapters, individuals with higher levels of evaluative well-being are more likely to have positive attitudes about the future, and those same attitudes seem to provide insurance/resilience against negative shocks (Binder and Coad, 2015; Graham and Nikolova, 2015.

Novel neuroscience work supports the direction of the research in economics and psychology. Different parts of the brain seem to react to hedonic versus long-term well-being. Studies reviewed by Davidson and Schuyler (2015) suggest that longer term (evaluative) well-being is associated with a more resilient response to adversity, operationalized by some as faster recovery following negative events. Parts of the brain and neurons commonly associated with positive affect and reward show connectivity with the region of the brain associated with regulation and goal-directed behavior. Depressed patients differ from controls on these measures. These neural patterns predict not only well-being reports but also peripheral biological measures (such as cortisol output) that may reflect both psychological and physical well-being.

Mindfulness, meanwhile, is a new concept in science that is linked to higher levels of well-being. "Well-being has been found to be elevated when individuals are better able to sustain positive emotion; recover more quickly from negative experiences; engage in empathic and altruistic acts; and express high levels of mindfulness" (Davidson and Schuyler, 2015, pp. 1065–1070).

The neural circuits that underlie each of these four constituents are partially separable, although there is some overlap. The prefrontal cortex and ventral striatum are especially important for sustained positive emotion; the connection between the prefrontal cortex and amygdala is a key node for recovery from negative events; anterior insula regions of the anterior cingulate cortex are implicated in empathetic response; and prefrontal cortex-ventral striatum are critical in altruistic behavior. And default networks that can be detected at rest are associated in mind-wandering versus mindfulness. Resilience seems to be part of this story as well: participants with higher scores on purpose in life are more resilient to negative events (in experiments). Empathy and altruism are also associated with higher levels of well-being, and there are again some signs of neural correlates.

In short, while this is a novel area, there is sufficient and growing evidence to suggest that higher levels of well-being and optimism about the future are correlated with behavioral outcomes of interest, many of which hinge on the ability to invest in the future rather than simply living in the present. The latest developments in well-being measurement make clear distinctions between hedonic (daily experience) and evaluative (life-course) dimensions, and as such provide an additional opportunity for research to explore how the different dimensions relate to future outlooks, time preferences, and individual behaviors.

While some of these traits are surely determined innately, part of the story is, no doubt, grounded in circumstances and repeated experiences. My research with Nikolova (Graham and Nikolova, 2015) and Lora (Graham and Lora, 2009), respectively, suggests that respondents emphasize each of these dimensions differently because of their capabilities and abilities to plan for and determine their futures. The very poorest typically focus on the daily experience dimension of well-being, as they do not have the luxury of longer time horizons (which may in part determine whether they have low levels of internal locus of control). This contrasts strongly with the perspective of those with greater capabilities and life choices. Thus when respondents with more means are asked about their own lives and well-being, they are more likely to think about their lives as a whole—the evaluative dimension.

This difference shows up in the data when specific questions pertaining to each dimension are included. The above-cited Kahneman and Deaton (2010) work shows that not having enough means is bad for both dimensions of well-being, but after a certain point more money does not make daily experience better. In contrast, the correlation between income and evaluative well-being continues up to the highest levels of income. This is because people with more income have greater capacity to lead the kinds of lives that they desire.

Our look at the differences in well-being—across dimensions and quintiles—in the United States, discussed in Chapter 3, confirms the general direction of these findings, with richer cohorts more likely to believe that effort and hard work will pay off in the future, and poorer cohorts more likely to experience daily stress. Our work on stress in Chapter 4 suggests that stress that is associated with circumstances beyond individuals' control is far worse for well-being than stress experienced by individuals with higher levels of income and education, as the latter is often associated with goal achievement rather than negative shocks. My work with Lora (Graham and Lora, 2009) on Latin America finds that friends and family are critical to the day-to-day survival challenges faced by the poor and represent the most important variable to their reported well-being, while work and health are the most important variables for respondents with more means, as these things give them the capacity to make choices about the kinds of lives that they want to lead.

Sendhil Mullainathan and Eldar Shafir (2013) show that scarcity creates a distinct psychology for everyone struggling to manage with less than they need, with several manifestations, most important the inability to plan well. Stress can limit attention, resulting in an emphasis on habitual behaviors at the expense of goal-oriented ones (Haushofer and Fehr, 2014). This applies not just to poor people, meanwhile. Busy people fail to manage their time efficiently for the same reasons the poor and those maxed out on credit cards fail to manage their money. The dynamics of scarcity reveal why dieters find it hard to resist temptation, why students and busy executives mismanage their time, and why the same sugarcane farmers are smarter after harvest than before.

Meanwhile, giving the poor (in poor countries) modest productive assets (such as ownership of a cow), combined with training and coaching, seems to produce remarkably positive effects. The authors of this research posit that an important if difficult factor to observe driving their result is the introduction of hope and positive expectations for the future to previously destitute people (Banerjee et al., 2015).

Along the same lines, but based on work on the poor in the United States, Crystal Hall, Jiaying Zhao, and Eldar Shafir (2014) focus on loss of personal efficacy, which in part comes from the stigma associated with being poor. In general, it can result in cognitive distancing, lower cognitive performance, and lack of take-up of beneficial programs. The authors conducted an experiment introducing self-affirmation among low-income individuals at an inner-city soup kitchen. Due to the generally low literacy levels of the participants, they used an oral rather than written affirmation procedure, in which participants were asked to describe an experience that made them feel successful or proud. Compared with participants who were not asked to think positively about themselves, the affirmed individuals performed better on a number of tasks, reflecting better executive control, higher fluid intelligence, and a greater willingness to avail themselves of benefit programs. Robustness tests revealed that the results were not driven by elevated positive mood, and the same intervention did not affect the performance of wealthy participants.

Identities and aspirations can be manipulated; they also seem to have persistent effects on behavior, both in experiments and in the real world. Jeffrey Butler's (2014) work on inequality beliefs, cited in earlier chapters, highlights how being persistently treated unfairly (in terms of unequal pay for performing the same task at the same level) translates into ability beliefs, with the lower paying groups believing that they have less ability and the higher paying ones believing they have greater ability, even though that is not the case.

Daphna Oyserman's extensive work on identities and adolescent performance in school finds that being part of a peer group that is deemed successful, believing that tasks are achievable, and having a vision for the future (which can be as simple as a family savings account dedicated to college) all make major differences in performance and completion of critical education levels. Robert Putnam's (2015) latest work on intergenerational mobility in the United States highlights the loss of personal efficacy among low-income cohorts as an explanatory factor in things such as unwanted pregnancies, and how that loss of efficacy is passed on from parents to children.

The work of Shanahan and coauthors (2014), described in Chapter 3, resonates here, and highlights how higher SES kids are more likely to inherit positive personality traits, even though they play a more important role in substituting for human capital investments for the future performance of low SES kids. Higher SES parents may foster these traits more and/or the opportunity structures of high SES kids may support certain traits, such as trust, agreeableness, and efficacy. Venator and Reeves (2015a) also find that the distribution of soft skills closely follows the income distribution, likely because these skills are often developed early in the education process, as in preschool, and low-income children are much less likely to have access to preschool as well as to have parents with those skills.

Individuals who are unable to have long-term time horizons, due to limited means and education, cognitive difficulties, discrimination, stigma, and associated stress, often fail to take up opportunities because they do not have enough faith in or vision of the future to believe that they will pay off. Jeremy Barofsky's (2015) work on AIDS-prevention interventions in Malawi and of subsidized health insurance under the ACA expansion in the United States finds that short time horizons and inconsistent time preferences play an important role in lack of take-up. In the United States he also finds that perceived stigma surrounding programs plays an additional negative role, and that having a friend or relative in the program plays a positive one (social networks may help alleviate information constraints and/or provide positive role models).

Kendall Swenson's (2015) work on the negative well-being effects of receiving transfer payments in the United States (discussed in Chapter 4) highlights the role of stigma and stress, both of which are associated with dealing with the administration of transfer programs for the poor, which are typically much less user-friendly than those of universal programs, such as social security and Medicare. There is also the role of unpredictability and inability of planning ahead, a channel that is highlighted in his findings on the negative effects associated with receiving transfers from private sources—such as charity, friends, and family—as opposed to from government programs (discussed in greater detail in Chapter 4).

Our Ongoing and Future Research

There is still, of course, a great deal that we do not know about these beliefs and behavior channels—including their causal directions. There are also some glimmers of hope in the story of unequal hopes and outcomes, such as the unusual levels of optimism among poor blacks compared to their counterparts. A better understanding of what drives that optimism and how or if it is associated with different behaviors pertaining to the future is an important topic for future research—and for the state of the American Dream.

As a part of that research going forward, we will also explore whether the 2009 financial crisis—which produced an exogenous shock to the well-being of all cohorts—differed in its effects on poor cohorts of different races. We will also build on our initial work on the role of local levels of inequality and see the extent to which it played a role—or not—in the well-being effects of that shock. Our findings on lower levels of social support in more unequal places suggest that at the least, the social support mechanisms for weathering such shocks are weaker in more unequal places.

Another important question is the extent to which attitudes about the future both matter to decisions about the future and can be changed to encourage behavioral changes that could enhance the futures of disadvantaged cohorts. These include investments in health and education and refraining from behaviors that are bad for long-term health outcomes, such as smoking and overeating on the one hand, and the take-up of new opportunities on the other. Jeremy Barofsky and I are beginning some experimental work designed to explore this, based on data from both the United States and Peru. The comparative data will allow us to explicitly explore if these channels operate in the same manner in contexts characterized by relative income differences, such as in the United States, versus absolute income poverty, as in Peru.

For the United States, we are using the Understanding America Study (UAS), a nationally representative Internet panel survey administered by the Center for Economic and Social Research at USC. The panel has over two thousand individuals who are queried frequently on sociodemographic and economic characteristics. We will include new questions on perceptions of opportunity, life control, and stress, explore variation over the income distribution, and investigate perceptions of the benefits of future-oriented decisions in the domains of health, education, and savings (via responses to statements such as "I believe getting a college education can lead to a good paying job"). Over a two-year period, we plan to assess how perceptions of opportunity and perceived benefits of future-oriented behaviors translate into actual decision making regarding health (use of preventive care, smoking, alcohol use), education (continued school enrollment), and saving, as well as how or if these outcomes vary across race and income cohorts.

As noted throughout the book, the psychological stresses associated with poverty decrease cognitive capacity and restrict opportunities. We will explicitly examine this question in a subset of UAS low-income respondents, testing the hypothesis that interventions that increase hope can change beliefs about the future and associated investments. We will first assess respondents' beliefs about the returns to education and their expected life expectancy. A random half will then be given information on the mobility prospects of those with a given education level in their area. We will then reassess beliefs for all respondents to see if the positive information intervention had an impact on beliefs.

In Peru, we are testing whether informational interventions affect aspirations and future-oriented decisions, as well as whether the impact of this intervention is mediated by absolute poverty. The experiment will target individuals with socioeconomic profiles that put them on the edge of eligibility for that nation's conditional cash transfer program, Juntos. We will again implement informational interventions to shift perceptions about the returns to education and preventive health behaviors. Again, we will compare the effect of the informational intervention for those who are similar sociodemographically, but in this case with one group below an absolute poverty line while the other is not.

In theory, the impact of the intervention should be larger for those in the poorer group. In practice, this work is at a very preliminary stage and we are not in a position to report the results. It is our hope, however, that exploring the role of an exogenous intervention that affects only half the sample of similar respondents can help us contribute to the experimental work cited above that explores (if not fully resolving) the causality question in the beliefs and behaviors channel. If we indeed find that altering aspirations can influence future behaviors, as did the Banerjee et al., Hall et al., and Butler experiments cited above, our results will contribute to a nascent body of evidence showing that hopes and aspirations are a genuine part of the diagnostic of poverty traps—and potentially their solution—in both rich and poor countries.

Guns and Fad Diets versus BabyBjörns and Machu Picchu

This chapter reviewed novel yet extensive evidence on the linkages between beliefs and behaviors, and how those links are mediated by time horizons and preferences, and related attitudes about the future. A wide range of research from various disciplines finds that there are differences in the well-being and outcomes of those individuals who have the capacity to envision, plan for, and invest in their futures and those who do not. Some of this capacity is clearly determined by the socioeconomic circumstances individuals are born into; some is determined by innate character traits and also by attitudes passed on from parents to children. This capacity seems to matter not only to positive outcomes, but to the ability to weather negative shocks and other forms of resilience.

In contrast, individuals who are consumed with daily struggles and living at the moment not only have less capacity to invest in their futures and less resilience in the face of negative shocks, but are less likely to take up incentives or opportunities when offered, because of low expectations, persistent beliefs, and/or other cognitive channels related to a combination of endowments and experiences.

Some of our early work over a decade ago, based on panel data, showed that individuals with higher levels of well-being and more faith in future mobility actually have better outcomes, both income and health related, findings that were at the time supported by those of psychological studies following the same individuals over time. Since then a range of new empirical and experimental work in economics, psychology, and sociology, as well as neuroscience, also supports the direction of the findings.

There is strong evidence of very large differences in time horizons and attitudes about the future across socioeconomic cohorts in the United States. There is some evidence, although less, of the linkages with behavioral outcomes. These findings provide a different kind of evidence for the Gatsby curve hypothesis of children's mobility being determined by their parents' circumstances. These beliefs tend to be persistent, and the children of cohorts with short time horizons and high discount rates thus are behind from the start compared to those of individuals who believe in and make extensive investments in their futures, in part because they have greater capacity to.

These findings are reflected, simply but strikingly, by the very different words that are common to people in difficult versus easy places to live, as Leonhardt's (2015) social media study found: guns, stress, diabetes, hell, and short-term fixes like fad diets and video games on the one hand; baby joggers, BabyBjörn, foam rollers, exotic travel destinations, and other investments in knowledge and health on the other.

While we have extensive data for the United States and the world in the Gallup surveys, they do not follow the same people over time. As such, in our research to date we have not been able to explore current beliefs and future outcomes in the same way that we could with panel data. We have, however, been able to explore the drivers of optimism about the future across socioeconomic, racial, and age cohorts.

We have found stark and worrisome levels of desperation among poor whites—indeed much more than any other socioeconomic or racial cohort. These trends are also mirrored in new findings on increasing mortality rates among uneducated middle-aged whites, which are driven by suicide, drug addiction, and alcohol poisoning—clear markers of desperation and lack of hope. At the same time, we found a surprising amount of optimism about the future among poor blacks—indeed they were the most optimistic group in all of our cohort analysis.

These trends reflect a drop in perceived status of low-skilled white workers. There has also been a narrowing of black-white wage and education gaps. And the happiness gap between blacks and whites has also continued to narrow, with black life satisfaction increasing more relative to white life satisfaction. Objective trends are clearly part of the story, but so are differential aspirations. Several new studies of well-being across racial cohorts support our findings and, in particular, highlight higher levels of resilience and hope among poor blacks and older blacks (of all income levels).

In sum, while there are surely nuances, the differences across poor and rich attitudes and faith in the future are increasingly driven by socioeconomic differences rather than by racial differences and discrimination related to those differences. While the latter is a positive story, the former is a cause for concern, as significant cohorts are compromised in their ability to envision, plan for, and invest in their futures, and this lack of hope is evident in the causes and trends of mortality for these cohorts.

Our new and ongoing research, which is based on panel data and experiments, is attempting to explore the relationship between current beliefs and future outcomes more explicitly, as well as how or if it varies across racial and socioeconomic cohorts. We are also testing to see if it can be altered via informational interventions that shift aspirations, interventions that, if successful, could be incorporated into existing policies.

Indeed, while the problems are complex and many of the solutions are long-term ones, there are still many issues that could be influenced by the right policies. The positive effects of the Moving to Opportunity program for those who move below a certain age as well as the positive effects on the life satisfaction—and hope—of mothers are cases in point. The stigmatizing effects of our transfer programs compared to those in other countries, which focus on encouraging the poor to invest in their future and to be more productive—and included—members of society, are another. And we clearly have much more to learn from the few glimmers of hope that we have—such as the surprising levels of optimism among poor blacks, and the extent to which simple interventions provide hope that leads to changes in long-term behaviors.

Tracking well-being trends on a more consistent basis—as many other countries are already doing, would at the very least mean that we would not be caught so much by surprise at the depth of desperation among important sectors of our society. Better awareness of such trends within and/or across cohorts might help prevent some of their worst manifestations from occurring. The challenges—and prospects—for policies to repair the American Dream for all Americans are the subject of the final chapter.

CHAPTER 6

Can We Save the Dream?

But I, being poor, have only my dreams;
I have spread my dreams under your feet;
Tread softly because you tread on my dreams.
                    —*William Butler Yeats,* "He Wishes for the Cloths of Heaven"

All of the chapters in this book have told the same story—albeit in slightly different ways—about the state of American society today. It is a story of two Americas, divided by vast differences in income; in education, health, and social insurance; in the kinds of lives individuals lead; and, most important, in hope and aspirations for future lives.

I have used a wide range of metrics, including standard economic measures of income inequality and mobility; measures of how much people smile, experience stress and worry, and have hope; econometric equations; figures, graphs, and maps; and stories based on words used in social media. Regardless of the metrics, the story is the same. In one America, opportunities remain endless, investments in education and hard work tend to pay off, and the capacity to make those investments is very high. In another America, belief in opportunity, education, and hard work is tattered, and most individuals lack confidence that investments in their future will pay off, much less the capacity to make them. The lives of these two separate Americas are characterized by starkly different markers of well-being, ranging from health status and mortality rates to daily experiences of pain, stress, and anger, the capacity to make long-term decisions, and levels of reported satisfaction with life and hope for the future.

The gap between the two Americas, meanwhile, seems to have undermined the sense of collective responsibility that underlies most social welfare systems. For many of those who have gotten ahead in rich America, it is convenient to believe that the poor are poor because it is their own fault. For many of those who have fallen behind, there is little sense that the rest of society cares. Our social welfare system, with its strong focus on individual responsibility, accentuates these differences, stigmatizing recipients of assistance rather than using it as a means to draw them back into society and to encourage them to invest in the health and education of their children. In Robert Putnam's words, we have "privatized" risk.

There are many outcomes that reflect the "two Americas" gap. One is a volatile political environment with support for antisystem politicians claiming magical paths to a return to a time when America was "great." Widening differentials in high school and college completion rates, with high rates of drop out by low-income students, are another. High levels of violence, suicide, and drug addiction among some low-education cohorts are perhaps the most tragic one. There are many others described throughout the book. These are difficult problems to solve, with a number of interacting and long-term causes, and there are no magic bullets. It is all too tempting to ignore the losers in the process as "nobodies" (as in chapter 4 epigraph).

Yet that is not an acceptable solution for a society that has long been a beacon of democratic government and free markets and that is, in the end, a nation settled by immigrants—both past and present. A more serious erosion of the American Dream could have reverberations well beyond the United States, the magnitude of which we cannot predict. While U.S. distributive trends are perhaps the starkest, increases in inequality are not unique to America. Most of the world's countries are integrated into the global economy and face many of the same structural trends (although, as noted throughout the book, many have more extensive social welfare and social support systems).

What, then, can be done? It is easy to blame politics or immigrants or globalization and to get people angry. It provides solace, on some level, to blame villains in the face of intractable social problems. Yet it does not solve the problems and may make them worse.

An alternative is to focus on what has worked and attempt to scale up those efforts, something that also requires more political consensus. The latter may (or may not) be a realistic objective after the fractious debate surrounding the

2016 elections has passed. Such efforts cross everything from early childhood education interventions to encouraging people to take up health insurance, giving individuals hope or enhanced self-esteem through affirmations, and/ or modest asset transfers. There are many examples of policies that work, and as many if not more experimental programs that have great potential to work.

As I have highlighted throughout the book, well-being metrics give us a new perspective on the problem and new ways to evaluate the potential solutions. They give us a new tool to evaluate whether interventions have changed daily living experiences and quality of life, such as stress, smiling, and access to social support on the one hand, and life satisfaction and ex- pectations for the future on the other. They also allow us to monitor the effects of interventions at different stages in the process, providing oppor- tunities for course correction. An additional advantage of the metrics is that the average person seems to engage more easily with measures that relate to individual happiness and emotions than with more complex—and distant— metrics of income inequality.

Can Policies Work? What Role for Well-Being Metrics?

The disparities in the kinds of lives that rich and poor individuals in the United States—and their children—lead are clear from the book. Address- ing them requires a range of approaches. There are many scholars who are more qualified than I to propose specific policies that could begin to solve this complex set of problems (see, for example, the AEI-Brookings report on poverty and opportunity, 2015). Instead, in what follows, I highlight a range of policies that have had success or have the potential to have success, and focus on how understanding and including the beliefs and behaviors channel might enhance the potential of many.

First of all, while finding villains is not the solution, raising awareness of the problem so that politicians cannot avoid it is a critical part of it. While inequality is finally entering the public discourse, public understanding of its causes and implications—and of the metrics that are used to measure it— is extremely low and subject to manipulation by politicians and the press. Well-being metrics, in contrast, are quite simple and easy for laypeople to understand. Knowing that the American Dream is unequally shared and that the poor experience much more pain and stress and anger and much less optimism about the future than the rich may well resonate with the public in a way comparisons of Gini coefficients across states or MSAs will not. Using these new data to raise awareness and understanding is, in the end, one of the main objectives of this book.

The potential policy solutions range from macro and structural ones, such as tax and regulatory policy and the role of unions, to micro ones, such as family and community programs, early education programs, the funding of different kinds of education, and spatial policies that emphasize the role of place and provide families with the opportunity to move to neighborhoods with better education and opportunities. I describe some examples here to highlight the range of ways in which inequality of incomes and, more important, of opportunities can be addressed.

In the macro area, there are many options, although they range in terms of their political feasibility. Anthony Atkinson (2015) advocates more progressive tax structures, more generous unemployment programs (including training), a more active government role in the arena of technological development, and a capital endowment or "minimum inheritance" paid to each citizen upon reaching adulthood (adjusted downward for those with higher incomes). Any or all of these policies would begin to address the problem, although they would not solve it on their own. Nor are many of them very feasible in the current divided U.S. political climate and its notoriously low support for progressive taxation. That said, if awareness is not raised by the discussion of different potential policy options, the agenda on inequality will never move forward. Putting a range of policy options on the table for discussion is an important first step toward some of them coming to fruition.

Robert Putnam (2015) focuses on four critical micro/behavioral-level areas: family structure, parenting, school, and community. His proposals include expanding EITC and protecting existing antipoverty programs; providing more generous parental leaves and better child care programs and state-funded preschool; equalizing public school funding, providing more community-based neighborhood schools, and increasing support for vocational high school programs/community colleges; ending pay-to-play extracurricular activities in public schools; and developing mentorship programs that tie schools to communities and community organizations.

None of these should be particularly politically controversial, which is one advantage of his approach. All of them should also enhance individual- and community-level well-being as well as opportunities. The focus on vocational schools addresses the gap in opportunities for members of society who do not have higher levels of education and the skills necessary to work in high-earning economic sectors. There will always be some members of society who either cannot reach higher levels of education and/or are unlikely to benefit from doing so, yet they can be productive members of society, and their chances of doing so depend in part on vocational skills and in part on earning decent wages after those skills are attained. Putnam's proposals reflect the fact that while education is a key factor, it cannot alone solve the deep-seated disparities in endowments, environments, experiences, and hope.

A major and very challenging issue, meanwhile, which relates to virtually all of these areas, is the tight linkage between family income and children's cognitive and noncognitive skills. Both sets of skills are critical to getting ahead in today's economy. David Autor's extensive research (summarized in Edsall, 2015) highlights the close relationship between the growth in men's and women's wages from 1963 to 2012 and their level of education. At the top end, there was a near doubling of wages in inflation-adjusted dollars for those with postgraduate degrees, while there was an actual decline in wages for those without high school diplomas at the bottom end. As of 2013, 66.5 percent of Americans did not have college degrees. Autor, among other authors, warns that the growth in disparities between "low" and "high" households, measured in terms of income, quality of schools, and neighborhoods, has the potential to reduce social mobility by providing highly unequal life chances for kids who might otherwise fare relatively similarly if born into similar environments.

Another example of the gaps in the skills that are passed on in low-income versus high-income families comes from the Early Childhood Longitudinal Study by the National Center for Education Statistics. The average cognitive ability score of kids from the bottom income quintile is 0.7 standard deviations below the mean, while it is 0.7 STDs above the mean for those in the top quintile. There is a similar pattern for noncognitive skills. Joana Venator and Richard Reeves (2015a) find that character, diligence, grit, self-control, creativity, and capacity to delay gratification all vary tremendously by income. Of those in the bottom quintile, 35 percent always or sometimes score low in these skills while 14.8 percent in the top do; 30 percent of those in the bottom sometimes or always score high compared to 48.3 percent of those in the top. With today's economic structure, a high school graduate with basic literacy and numeracy skills alone cannot easily obtain a stable middle-class job, as the value of analytical, technological, communication, and teamwork skills has been accentuated in the past fifteen years.

Education is fundamental but has limited potential to solve two major problems. As Kearney and Levine (2015) note, increasing the number of college graduates would lower the inequalities in the bottom half of the distribution by pulling up earnings, but would not address the biggest gaps between high earners and those with high skills and the rest (a gap that vocational training can narrow but not undo). The second issue is that even good schools—including charter schools—cannot solve the problems of children who come from and go back to dysfunctional families, with no expectations. There are countless examples throughout the book of how identities, task relevance, and interventions that change aspirations can make a difference to these problems at the margin. We still have a long way to go before we understand how to inspire hope and aspirations among those whose life experiences have precluded their existence; we have to begin to do so (and our research going forward, described in Chapter 5, is a part of that effort).

While this is a difficult challenge, there are interventions that work and that change hopes and aspirations. Moving to Opportunity is one example that showed the importance of place and the timing of interventions. Children—particularly boys—who moved to better neighborhoods with better schools earlier (before their teen years) benefited far more from the program than those who moved later, for example (Chetty, Hendren, and Katz, 2015). Suggestive of the hope channel, meanwhile, the very early interventions of MTO did not detect differences in children's outcomes (likely because it was too early) but did find increases in the subjective well-being of the mothers who moved (Ludwig et al., 2012), and their higher levels of life satisfaction may have played a role in the ultimate outcomes. More recent research by Magdalena Bendini (2015) based on the Young Lives panel survey in Peru, which follows children born in the new millennium through their teens, finds that maternal mental health is significantly associated with young children's nutritional and educational outcomes.

There are other experiments. One of these is the Perry Project, from 1962 to 1967 in Ypsilanti, Michigan. Of 123 low-income, low-IQ kids ages three to four, 58 were assigned to intensive, 2.5-hour sessions five days a week for preschool training; the others were not. In evaluating the project, Jim Heckman and coauthors (cited in Edsall, 2015) report that while the project did not increase long-term IQ, it did raise achievement test scores. Personality skills can enhance learning and then achievement test scores; indeed 30 to 40 percent of the explained variance in scores across students was due to personality traits and not cognitive skills.

There are also specific labor market proposals that can address the gap in educational and vocational skills for those who do not benefit from early interventions. Harry Holzer's (2015) work on improving CTE (vocational education) suggests the need for more resources to community colleges, starting with rewarding K–12 efforts to push and prepare the relevant students to this track. At present, community colleges do not have the resources to make this work. There is a lot of enrollment and a lot of drop out. Holzer's work also suggests the importance of encouraging employers to create more "good" jobs that allow low-income workers to learn in and stay in their jobs (via benefits such as sick leave and maternity leave). Tax credits, technical assistance on human resource issues, moral suasion, and government contracting preference are all potential tools. Again, this research suggests the importance of addressing noncognitive skills and the stress/uncertainty/hope channel as well as learning.

In this arena it is also important to address the specific problem of the "missing men": young men and boys of color (Spaulding et al., 2015). This group faces a double-edged sword of lack of training, geographic issues, absence of educational guidance, and higher incarceration rates, in addition to discrimination. These problems often begin early, via low expectations in schools. While the very high unemployment rates (30 percent) for African American men (vs. 14 percent for Hispanic young men) in the 1980s dropped in the 1990s, employment and earnings have dropped again for both black and Hispanic young men since 2000. These statistics also beg the question of the extent to which these "missing men" are accurately captured in the data that highlight optimism among poor blacks, for example.

There are other related problems, such as the need for assistance for low-income, low-education individuals going from education system to training opportunities to the labor market. As much research has shown, in the absence of confidence or faith in the future, they may not exploit these opportunities. There is a role here for mentoring interventions, for faith- or community-based groups, and the like. Again, this is an area where well-being metrics are useful for both program design and monitoring outcomes, and where better understanding of the potential role of interventions that increase aspirations would be extremely helpful.

Another major issue is the stigma innate in U.S. welfare policy. As discussed in Chapters 4 and 5, welfare recipients in the United States are stigmatized in ways that recipients of universal programs (like Medicare and Social Security) are not, and they have lower levels of well-being because of it. In contrast, the highly successful conditional cash transfer programs in Latin America hinge on giving poor individuals the opportunity to make adult choices about the use of received income, rather than in-kind transfers, but these are conditional on their investing in their children's future via health and education (for a review, see Parker and Todd, forthcoming). Some studies have also shown that these programs improve the subjective well-being of recipients (Chindarkar, 2012). The very strong U.S. focus on individual effort and success, which has worked remarkably well for those with the luck, skills, and endowments that allow them to succeed, has also resulted in a tendency to stigmatize those who fail.

At least in theory (and with plenty of evidence in practice, as noted above), social welfare policies that focus on pulling people up and into society and helping them to be productive, rather than highlighting their failures, are more effective. Food stamps in the United States are case in point, both because of the stigma surrounding them and because they do not pull people up or link to anything greater or future oriented. They are simply about surviving the day with another meal or a minimum stipend.

The role of luck in success, meanwhile, has been underplayed in our public language and knowledge, and as a result the achievements of "winners" tend to be overly attributed to hard work and skills, while the failures of losers tend to be overly attributed to lack of those things. Yet luck often plays a major role in individual success stories, from the rags-to-riches stories by Horatio Alger to finding a life-changing mentor in college or having a risky investment pay off.

Robert Frank (2016) describes how, in a world increasingly dominated by winner-take-all markets, chance opportunities and trivial initial advantages often translate into much larger ones—and enormous income differences— over time. He highlights the fact that false beliefs about luck persist (and vary across the political spectrum in expected ways) and that myths about individual success stories shape individual and political choices in harmful ways. A good example from the 2016 elections is the extent to which Donald Trump has been able to convince his supporters that he has pulled himself up by the boot straps, in the style of an Alger hero, while underplaying the role of luck—such as the money that he inherited from his father—in the process. While policies cannot address luck explicitly, better understanding of its role in success and failure might lead to a more inclusive and constructive dialogue about those who fall behind.

The EITC program is an exception to most U.S. welfare programs, as it links assistance to labor market participation. The views and attitudes that were reviewed in Chapter 3 highlight big differences in support for minimum wage and other work-oriented support versus TANF and food stamps. This is in part because of lack of trust in the government, but in part it is because it is seen as "us" versus "them": handouts to the poor in contrast to a minimum wage for "workers." EITC recipients themselves report that they do not think of the program as a "handout," and find it an important buffer against the fear and stress related to having a positive tax liability each year. The lump sum nature of the transfer (an average of $2,359 per recipient), meanwhile, precludes it from being used for day-to-day consumption needs throughout the year; instead, families receiving the EITC typically use it to pay off their debts or for mobility-"enhancing" purchases such as cars for travel to work or education investments (surveys of EITC recipients cited in Rodrigues and Sawhill, 2015).

Despite the success of EITC (and potential programs like it), however, which may be effective for many of the poor, the plight of those individuals who are in either very unstable jobs and/or other dire straits and are not eligible for EITC remains a concern. Such individuals—who often have associated mental health issues—may also fail to qualify (or apply) for other transfers, and fall even further off the grid (as discussed in Chapter 4).

Well-Being Metrics

Measuring the well-being of different socioeconomic and racial cohorts, and how it is influenced (or not) by particular policies, is yet another potential input into this complex equation. Much of the book has focused on the extent to which aspirations and hope for the future influence current behaviors and investments in the future (or not), including the take-up of policies that are designed to enhance future opportunities and security. A first-order step is to document baseline trends in well-being (across its two major dimensions) and related attitudes. That would be a relatively inexpensive means to provide early assessments of potential problems as well as of interventions and policies designed to solve them.

As noted above, some of the earliest assessments of Moving to Opportunity found no effects on children's attitudes but did find life satisfaction increases among the mothers who moved. Provision of hope for the mothers, meanwhile, is a plausible channel via which the program ultimately improved children's outcomes. At the same time, as the Bendini (2015) research suggests, better tracking of mothers' well-being in general could help identify mental distress and possibly alleviate the associated costs for the outcomes of their children.

Well-being metrics are increasingly being utilized by policy makers and practitioners. The Behavioral Insights Team in the cabinet office of the British government has provided a wealth of experience along these lines (Behavioral Insights Team, 2015), providing information on the costs or benefits of particular policies as assessed by well-being metrics with assessments based on traditional cost-benefit analysis. Legal scholars are also beginning to consider the use of these metrics as alternatives to those based on willingness-to-pay data, for example, in cost-benefit analysis (Graham, 2016). In both cases, traditional cost-benefit analysis misses important parts of the picture.

Many legal decisions about compensation are based on hypothetical willingness-to-pay questions, such as how many years of life an individual would trade for a riskier but higher paying job, or to not have lost a leg. Yet because of differential discount rates, financial limitations, and other factors, the poor are likely to accept greater risks for more money in answering these questions, while those who have not experienced an injury such as losing a leg can only hypothesize about what it is worth. Well-being metrics can complement these kinds of valuations with those based on comparing the life satisfaction levels of individuals with or without certain conditions and/or in different kinds of jobs, among other things.

The British experience suggests another example. Cost-benefit analysis suggested that closing rural post offices would be a good decision from a fiscal perspective, as they do not deliver much mail and are remote and expensive to maintain, and it was feasible to have mail delivered via another method. Yet the Behavioral Insights Team found, based on well-being metrics, that the visit to the rural post office was the most important time of the day for rural respondents, particularly elderly ones. The complementary information provided by well-being metrics resulted in a very different kind of cost-benefit calculation.

More generally, regular collection of metrics on trends in well-being, as the U.K. government is already doing and the OECD is recommending for national statistics offices around the world, would complement the income-based information that we regularly collect with GNP data, and would give us an institutionalized way to monitor trends over time and across cohorts. For example, had we been monitoring well-being trends in the United States over the past decade, we might not have been caught off guard by the extreme desperation among poor and near poor and uneducated whites. More timely awareness of high levels of misery or desperation among particular cohorts, for example, might help us avert worse outcomes, such as the high rates of suicide and drug addiction currently driving mortality rates among middle-aged whites.

At the international level, the metrics have been particularly effective at highlighting the extent to which different social, institutional, and environmental arrangements can translate into higher levels of well-being in countries of comparable levels of per capita income. Countries such as Costa Rica and Denmark score higher than their counterparts of similar income levels, while the United States scores lower than its income levels would predict, all else held equal (Helliwell, Layard, and Sachs, 2013). The metrics are also useful in assessing the effects of changes in the nature of economies and social safety nets. Arguably, awareness of the dramatic downward trends in life satisfaction associated with the Chinese economic transition in the 1990s might have helped avert the dramatic increase in suicide rates there at the time (Graham, Zhou, and Zhang, 2015).

Regular collection of well-being trends within the United States could provide useful insights into problematic trends that could then be averted or at least alleviated with targeted policies. Some cities and states in the United States—such as Santa Monica and Portland on the one hand, and Maryland and Vermont on the other—have already begun pilot efforts to collect information on the well-being of their populations as a way to inform policy and also to elicit civic engagement in efforts to improve community well-being (see, for example, Graham, 2015). As in the case of all of the other policies reviewed above, this is not a magic bullet, but it would provide critical information that could help issues such as deep desperation—and its manifestations—among particular socioeconomic and racial cohorts.

Restoring Hope

The most challenging component of all of this, and a main theme of the book, is the black box of no hope, low expectations, and little faith in the future. How do we deal with the bottoming out of the American Dream, with the desperate individuals at the bottom with low expectations, miserable life chances, and very high discount rates. These same cohorts also often have dysfunctional families, as many individuals have such high levels of stress and low levels of well-being that they are difficult to live with, and they pass on that stress and lack of hope to their children. How do we address the plight of the cohorts of Americans who have "lost the narrative of their lives"? How do you change expectations and beliefs?

Lack of hope and faith in the future may seem intangible and far from the realm of policy, but it is reflected in real-world outcomes. In the same way that those with higher levels of well-being and optimism about the future invest more in those futures and have better outcomes, those with no hope are living compromised and shorter lives. They have higher levels of stress and many other indicators of ill-being; they have lower levels of life expectancy; and they spend much of their lives living in the moment, dealing with daily stresses and struggles in whatever way they can. The recent increase in mortality rates for middle-aged, uneducated whites is a stark marker of this ill-being and lack of hope. Not surprisingly, the ability of such cohorts to support and invest in their children is severely compromised. And the further they fall behind their wealthier, healthier, and happier counterparts in society, the less attainable a bright future seems to be.

Indeed, the same cohorts that could most benefit from new incentives to improve their futures often fail to utilize those incentives because they simply don't believe that they will pay off. Examples in the book include the failure to take advantage of health care when offered or to complete college despite the existence of financial support, and beliefs in inferior ability merely because of visible and consistent inequality in rewards structures.

This is a depressing picture, and the American Dream is clearly tattered. Yet there are signs of hope, and we must find more. Some are in the success stories of programs that seem to work, such as Moving to Opportunity and the EITC. Some are in new experiments that show that very simple interventions that provide hope, such as the provision of a modest asset or simply affirmation and a more positive attitude, can make a difference to the subsequent performance of the poor or destitute. These interventions are as simple as providing cows to the poor in developing countries and affirmation and confidence building in soup kitchens. Of course these examples are just scratching the surface, and affirmation alone cannot solve a range of complex problems. Yet what we know about these interventions suggests that the beliefs and behaviors channel matters, that it can be altered, and that it can increase the odds of positive outcomes.

There are also some unexplained surprises in the story. One is the unexpected levels of optimism among poor blacks and Hispanics, which in part are a reflection of very gradually narrowing gaps in educational achievement between these groups and whites, at the same time that the achievement gaps across income groups have either increased or at least stayed the same (depending on education level). In part the optimism reflects differences in community and other support structures across racial and other cohorts. Better understanding these important pockets of hope is critical.

It is abundantly clear that without hope and faith in the future, individuals will fail to take up incentives and interventions even in instances where policy changes make them available. More research is necessary, of course. Yet the existing body of work shows why incentives fail: impatience and lack of faith in the future in the instance of health insurance, beliefs formed by unequal rewards, and the role of identity and relevance versus impossibility in the completion of tasks in the classroom also provide hints about how modest interventions can alter such beliefs. If beliefs can be formed in a simple experimental game setting, then they can likely, if more slowly, also be reversed in schools, communities, and beyond.

Interventions early in the life cycle are the most promising on this front (as in the MTO experiment), but they are not the only ones. Hope is not delimited by age. Indeed, much of the work on well-being and aging suggests that older individuals are not only more emotionally stable but more positive in general (Blanchflower and Oswald, 2008; Graham, 2005, 2009; Rauch, forthcoming). Our findings in Chapter 4 on hope and optimism among elderly blacks support this. Grandparents could ultimately play a role in reinforcing this channel for younger generations (and likely already do among some cohorts).

Policies that are crafted to address inequality might be more successful if those who have lost hope believe they have a future and can do better if they invest in that future. In other words, policies that encourage individual investments in things such as education must also convince potential recipients that they will pay off. As discussed in the book, there are myriad examples of lack of take-up of such interventions by disadvantaged cohorts. This is an area where our existing knowledge only scratches the surface. Yet we know that it matters.

We are seeing the consequences of lack of hope in rising suicide rates and addiction to opioids and other drugs, in crime and health care outcomes, and in differential educational attainment, among many other measurable outcomes. These are remarkable and alarming trends for one of the wealthiest countries in the world. Monitoring trends in well-being regularly going forward, meanwhile, may help us avert life-threatening behaviors among particularly desperate cohorts, as well as better understand those behaviors that are associated with optimism and higher expectations for the future.

These trends are in economic and other kinds of publicly available data, and they have begun to enter public debate. My objective in this book has been to shed insights on the same trends through well-being metrics, which the average person on the street seems to relate to more easily than to Gini coefficients or data on high school completion rates. They complement the traditional income-based measures with a story of unequally shared hopes, dreams, happiness, and well-being. Not only do the metrics resonate in terms of people's understanding, but they also highlight the important link between beliefs, behaviors, and investments in the future. My personal hope is that the metrics that I have used to assess the state of the American Dream can play a role in restoring the pursuit of happiness for all.

Appendix

This appendix comprises the longer and more complex tables in the book. For Chapter 3, these include the means and standard deviations of the range of well-being measures in the chapter, as well as the quantile regressions for the United States and Latin America. For Chapter 4, these include the regressions on life satisfaction and future life satisfaction for the race and income cohorts and the race and age cohorts; those on good stress and bad stress for the United States and Latin America; and those on local level inequality and well-being and social support in the United States. While these tables may be too technical for the lay reader, they are important for those with an interest in the methods and detailed results underlying the discussion in both of these chapters. Comments and critique are, as always, welcome.

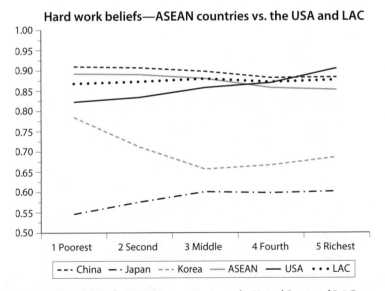

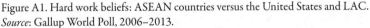

Figure A1. Hard work beliefs: ASEAN countries versus the United States and LAC.
Source: Gallup World Poll, 2006–2013.

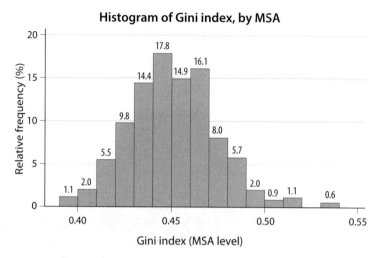

Figure A2. Distribution of inequality across MSAs.
Source: 2009–2013, 5-Year American Community Survey.
Note: This histogram depicts only the 348 MSAs for which there are observations for the variables of interest.

Table A1. Calculations based on Gallup World Poll 2005–2013

hhincq	year	LAC				USA				Difference: USA-LAC			
		bpl	stress	smile	wrkhrd	bpl	stress	smile	wrkhrd	bpl	stress	smile	wrkhrd
1 Poorest	2006	4.9295	0.3021	0.7347	0.8191	6.3598	0.4684	0.6383	0.7513	1.4303	0.1664	-0.0964	-0.0678
2 Second	2006	5.1725	0.3419	0.7400	0.8519	6.9898	0.4643	0.7704	0.7887	1.8173	0.1224	0.0304	-0.0632
3 Middle	2006	5.4033	0.3217	0.7550	0.7735	7.4746	0.3613	0.8571	0.8655	2.0712	0.0396	0.1022	0.0920
4 Fourth	2006	5.7759	0.2892	0.7889	0.8208	7.4636	0.4253	0.8295	0.8812	1.6877	0.1361	0.0405	0.0604
5 Richest	2006	6.2109	0.2796	0.8206	0.7766	7.9595	0.4161	0.8707	0.8986	1.7485	0.1365	0.0501	0.1220
Difference: Q5-Q1		1.2815	-0.0225	0.0859	-0.0425	1.5997	-0.0523	0.2325	0.1473	0.3182	-0.0299	0.1465	0.1898
1 Poorest	2007	5.0878	0.2610	0.7810	0.8527	6.7429		0.7050	0.7941	1.6550		-0.0759	-0.0586
2 Second	2007	5.2903	0.2833	0.7995	0.8375	7.3130		0.7023	0.8077	2.0227		-0.0972	-0.0298
3 Middle	2007	5.7027	0.2730	0.8167	0.8360	7.3911		0.7965	0.8186	1.6884		-0.0203	-0.0174
4 Fourth	2007	6.1905	0.2701	0.8375	0.8467	7.5515		0.7606	0.8476	1.3610		-0.0769	0.0009
5 Richest	2007	6.5638	0.2530	0.8539	0.8475	7.9337		0.8398	0.8989	1.3699		-0.0141	0.0514
Difference: Q5-Q1		1.4759	-0.0080	0.0729	-0.0052	1.1908		0.1347	0.1048	-0.2851		0.0618	0.1099
1 Poorest	2008	5.0148	0.2789	0.7918	0.8328	6.2553	0.4709	0.6793	0.8571	1.2405	0.1920	-0.1125	0.0244
2 Second	2008	5.4379	0.2791	0.8207	0.8232	7.1618	0.3842	0.7892	0.8775	1.7239	0.1051	-0.0314	0.0542
3 Middle	2008	5.8867	0.2862	0.8226	0.8269	7.4667	0.3524	0.8606	0.8857	1.5799	0.0662	0.0380	0.0588
4 Fourth	2008	6.2291	0.2853	0.8382	0.8354	7.6975	0.4454	0.8235	0.9160	1.4683	0.1601	-0.0147	0.0806
5 Richest	2008	6.6180	0.2791	0.8615	0.8584	7.7534	0.4795	0.8219	0.9172	1.1354	0.2003	-0.0396	0.0589
Difference: Q5-Q1		1.6032	0.0002	0.0697	0.0256	1.4981	0.0086	0.1426	0.0601	-0.1051	0.0083	0.0729	0.0345

(continued)

Table A1. (*continued*)

hhincq	year	LAC				USA				Difference: USA-LAC			
		bpl	stress	smile	wrkhrd	bpl	stress	smile	wrkhrd	bpl	stress	smile	wrkhrd
1 Poorest	2009	5.6952	0.2978	0.8027	0.8137	6.5867	0.5133	0.7651	0.8562	0.8915	0.2155	-0.0376	0.0425
2 Second	2009	6.0310	0.2868	0.8269	0.8028	7.1452	0.5108	0.8118	0.8913	1.1142	0.2239	-0.0150	0.0885
3 Middle	2009	6.3539	0.2791	0.8396	0.8139	7.2192	0.4384	0.8082	0.9041	0.8653	0.1592	-0.0314	0.0902
4 Fourth	2009	6.5976	0.2710	0.8529	0.8228	7.4371	0.4096	0.7892	0.9146	0.8395	0.1386	-0.0637	0.0919
5 Richest	2009	6.9659	0.2533	0.8855	0.8244	8.1037	0.3841	0.8415	0.9571	1.1377	0.1308	-0.0441	0.1327
Difference: Q5-Q1		1.2707	-0.0445	0.0829	0.0107	1.5170	-0.1292	0.0764	0.1009	0.2463	-0.0847	-0.0065	0.0902
1 Poorest	2010	5.6057	0.2663	0.8052	0.8710	6.5478	0.4204	0.8194	0.9026	0.9420	0.1541	0.0141	0.0316
2 Second	2010	5.7454	0.2679	0.8305	0.9028	7.2609	0.4259	0.8333	0.8519	1.5155	0.1581	0.0028	-0.0510
3 Middle	2010	6.2596	0.2756	0.8440	0.8779	7.3857	0.4071	0.8500	0.9065	1.1261	0.1315	0.0060	0.0286
4 Fourth	2010	6.4827	0.2811	0.8543	0.8768	7.3780	0.4695	0.8841	0.8704	0.8953	0.1884	0.0299	-0.0064
5 Richest	2010	6.9184	0.2930	0.8575	0.8707	8.0167	0.4254	0.8956	0.9337	1.0982	0.1325	0.0381	0.0630
Difference: Q5-Q1		1.3127	0.0266	0.0523	-0.0003	1.4689	0.0050	0.0762	0.0311	0.1562	-0.0216	0.0239	0.0314
1 Poorest	2011	5.4233	0.3455	0.8091	0.8905	6.7854	0.4637	0.7765	0.8110	1.3621	0.1182	-0.0325	-0.0795
2 Second	2011	5.8324	0.3432	0.8451	0.8931	6.9808	0.4696	0.7889	0.8305	1.1484	0.1264	-0.0562	-0.0626
3 Middle	2011	6.1626	0.3368	0.8409	0.8924	7.3913	0.5046	0.7917	0.8451	1.2287	0.1677	-0.0492	-0.0473
4 Fourth	2011	6.3449	0.3494	0.8566	0.9023	7.5401	0.4355	0.8387	0.9012	1.1953	0.0861	-0.0179	-0.0011
5 Richest	2011	6.7715	0.3437	0.8828	0.8885	7.5920	0.4405	0.8024	0.8947	0.8205	0.0968	-0.0804	0.0063
Difference: Q5-Q1		1.3482	-0.0018	0.0737	-0.0020	0.8067	-0.0232	0.0259	0.0837	-0.5416	-0.0214	-0.0478	0.0858

Table A1. (continued)

hhincq	year	LAC				USA				Difference: USA-LAC			
		bpl	stress	smile	wrkhrd	bpl	stress	smile	wrkhrd	bpl	stress	smile	wrkhrd
1 Poorest	2012	5.6829	0.3797	0.7859	0.8661	6.6173	0.5140	0.7471	0.7816	0.9344	0.1343	-0.0387	-0.0845
2 Second	2012	5.8470	0.3594	0.8255	0.8999	6.9201	0.4235	0.8204	0.7929	1.0731	0.0642	-0.0051	-0.1070
3 Middle	2012	6.2098	0.3714	0.8363	0.8851	7.2952	0.4076	0.8109	0.8162	1.0854	0.0362	-0.0254	-0.0688
4 Fourth	2012	6.4847	0.3678	0.8420	0.8828	7.4422	0.4301	0.8770	0.8261	0.9574	0.0623	0.0350	-0.0567
5 Richest	2012	6.8397	0.3540	0.8748	0.8880	7.6907	0.4000	0.8730	0.8843	0.8510	0.0460	-0.0019	-0.0037
Difference: Q5-Q1		1.1568	-0.0257	0.0890	0.0220	1.0734	-0.1140	0.1258	0.1027	-0.0834	-0.0883	0.0369	0.0807
1 Poorest	2013	5.6494	0.3912	0.8061	0.8909	6.7035	0.5230	0.7241	0.8523	1.0541	0.1318	-0.0820	-0.0386
2 Second	2013	5.8662	0.3801	0.8172	0.8913	7.0968	0.5669	0.7564	0.7941	1.2306	0.1868	-0.0607	-0.0972
3 Middle	2013	6.1967	0.3513	0.8409	0.8918	7.3505	0.4744	0.8411	0.8595	1.1538	0.1231	0.0002	-0.0323
4 Fourth	2013	6.4590	0.3441	0.8577	0.8793	7.3110	0.4231	0.8125	0.8431	0.8520	0.0790	-0.0452	-0.0361
5 Richest	2013	6.7309	0.3201	0.8622	0.8754	7.5261	0.4137	0.8468	0.8496	0.7952	0.0935	-0.0154	-0.0258
Difference: Q5-Q1		1.0815	-0.0710	0.0561	-0.0155	0.8226	-0.1093	0.1226	-0.0027	-0.2589	-0.0383	0.0666	0.0128
1 Poorest	2006–2013	5.4459	0.3230	0.7950	0.8593	6.5766	0.4819	0.7295	0.8229	1.1307	0.1590	-0.0655	-0.0363
2 Second	2006–2013	5.7133	0.3185	0.8209	0.8644	7.0767	0.4614	0.7865	0.8340	1.3634	0.1428	-0.0343	-0.0303
3 Middle	2006–2013	6.0951	0.3162	0.8321	0.8612	7.3614	0.4253	0.8242	0.8579	1.2662	0.1091	-0.0079	-0.0034
4 Fourth	2006–2013	6.3876	0.3144	0.8472	0.8654	7.4685	0.4324	0.8201	0.8701	1.0809	0.1181	-0.0272	0.0047
5 Richest	2006–2013	6.7481	0.3042	0.8663	0.8635	7.7817	0.4201	0.8506	0.9058	1.0336	0.1159	-0.0157	0.0423
Difference: Q5-Q1		1.3022	-0.0187	0.0713	0.0042	1.2051	-0.0618	0.1211	0.0828	-0.0971	-0.0431	0.0498	0.0786

Table A2. Best possible life quantile regressions, United States

	(1)	(2)	(3)	(4)	(5)
	Q10	Q25	Q50	Q75	Q90
No health problem	1.266***	1.373***	0.797***	0.542***	0.215
	(0.241)	(0.275)	(0.194)	(0.155)	(0.252)
Belief in hard work	0.805**	0.654**	0.692**	0.659***	0.371
	(0.357)	(0.274)	(0.301)	(0.245)	(0.292)
Freedom	1.268**	0.613**	0.589**	0.347*	0.054
	(0.503)	(0.301)	(0.234)	(0.202)	(0.293)
Some college/college diploma	0.862***	0.356**	0.278***	0.096	−0.126
	(0.263)	(0.145)	(0.091)	(0.091)	(0.114)
Log household income	0.442***	0.473***	0.207**	0.028	0.041
	(0.108)	(0.076)	(0.096)	(0.068)	(0.059)
Employment categories (ref. group: out of the labor force)					
Full-time employee	0.050	−0.249	−0.292**	−0.321*	−0.397*
	(0.288)	(0.203)	(0.145)	(0.182)	(0.202)
Self-employed	0.030	−0.365	0.245	0.150	0.012
	(0.566)	(0.610)	(0.434)	(0.301)	(0.365)
Voluntary part-time	0.399	0.176	0.334	−0.109	−0.111
	(0.291)	(0.344)	(0.218)	(0.156)	(0.193)
Unemployed	−1.362**	−1.246***	−0.798**	−0.746**	−0.738*
	(0.636)	(0.376)	(0.361)	(0.299)	(0.385)
Involuntary part-time	−0.400	−0.376	−0.433	−0.451**	−0.115
	(0.343)	(0.457)	(0.320)	(0.201)	(0.368)
Smiled yesterday	1.221***	1.004***	0.722***	0.716***	0.567***
	(0.364)	(0.195)	(0.224)	(0.156)	(0.150)
Learned yesterday	0.503	0.498***	0.441***	0.308**	0.111
	(0.323)	(0.129)	(0.104)	(0.143)	(0.110)
Age	−0.076**	−0.048**	−0.056***	−0.039*	−0.016
	(0.033)	(0.024)	(0.018)	(0.021)	(0.021)
Age-squared/100	0.075**	0.051*	0.056***	0.043**	0.018
	(0.031)	(0.026)	(0.019)	(0.020)	(0.020)
Female	0.796***	0.321***	0.377***	0.172	−0.004
	(0.268)	(0.108)	(0.106)	(0.130)	(0.119)

Table A2. (*continued*)

	(1)	(2)	(3)	(4)	(5)
	Q10	**Q25**	**Q50**	**Q75**	**Q90**
Married or in civil partnership	0.053	0.133	0.210*	0.234	0.161
	(0.248)	(0.186)	(0.118)	(0.150)	(0.152)
Urban area	−0.298	−0.286*	−0.318***	−0.311**	−0.254**
	(0.284)	(0.147)	(0.117)	(0.124)	(0.121)
Child in household	−0.123	−0.173	−0.269**	−0.069	0.220
	(0.187)	(0.225)	(0.123)	(0.141)	(0.159)
Household size	0.031	0.004	−0.009	−0.025	−0.048
	(0.068)	(0.044)	(0.020)	(0.042)	(0.050)
Religion important	−0.089	−0.008	0.055	0.230**	0.281
	(0.161)	(0.132)	(0.130)	(0.112)	(0.196)
Year dummies	Yes	Yes	Yes	Yes	Yes
Observations	1,417	1,417	1,417	1,417	1,417
Pseudo-R^2	.185	.183	.088	.069	.045

Source: Gallup World Poll.

Note: All quantile regressions are for all available years of data for the 2009–2013 period and use bootstrapped standard errors (with 20 replications). Not all variables are available in all years. Household size data are not available for 2013. The dependent variable is BPL, which measures respondents' assessments of their current life relative to the best possible life they can imagine on a scale of 0 (*worst possible life*) to 10 (*best possible life*). Q10 corresponds to the 10 percent quantile, Q25 is the 25 percent quantile, Q50 is the 50 percent quantile (median), Q75 is the 75 percent quantile, and Q90 is the 90 percent quantile. Household income is log-transformed and in international dollars (ID), which allows comparisons across countries and time. The table reports the pseudo-R^2 for each quantile regression. Robust standard errors in parentheses.

*p < .1. **p < .05. ***p < .01.

Table A3. Best possible life quantile regressions, Latin America and the Caribbean

	(1)	(2)	(3)	(4)	(5)
	Q10	Q25	Q50	Q75	Q90
No health problem	0.722***	0.514***	0.501***	0.498***	0.236**
	(0.043)	(0.031)	(0.027)	(0.031)	(0.093)
Belief in hard work	0.257***	0.216***	0.258***	0.254***	0.194**
	(0.054)	(0.030)	(0.034)	(0.040)	(0.082)
Freedom	0.273***	0.239***	0.256***	0.278***	0.197***
	(0.038)	(0.025)	(0.027)	(0.025)	(0.070)
Some college/college diploma	0.592***	0.555***	0.524***	0.241***	−0.042
	(0.052)	(0.042)	(0.036) .	(0.035)	(0.027)
Log household income	0.467***	0.353***	0.211***	0.125***	0.017
	(0.018)	(0.011)	(0.011)	(0.012)	(0.014)
Employment categories (ref. group: out of the labor force)					
Full-time employee	0.196***	0.102***	0.079**	−0.003	−0.016
	(0.056)	(0.029)	(0.036)	(0.030)	(0.035)
Self-employed	−0.141***	−0.127***	−0.136***	−0.181***	−0.056
	(0.052)	(0.040)	(0.034)	(0.036)	(0.045)
Voluntary part-time	0.187***	0.047	−0.051	−0.081*	−0.031
	(0.064)	(0.039)	(0.049)	(0.049)	(0.040)
Unemployed	−0.656***	−0.500***	−0.524***	−0.552***	−0.205*
	(0.065)	(0.052)	(0.038)	(0.051)	(0.109)
Involuntary part-time	−0.245***	−0.264***	−0.269***	−0.312***	−0.172**
	(0.069)	(0.036)	(0.039)	(0.046)	(0.082)
Smiled yesterday	0.581***	0.483***	0.474*** ·	0.496***	0.559***
	(0.044)	(0.035)	(0.033)	(0.028)	(0.159)
Learned yesterday	0.336***	0.295***	0.349***	0.407***	0.175**
	(0.024)	(0.025)	(0.020)	(0.022)	(0.074)
Age	−0.059***	−0.050***	−0.054***	−0.058***	−0.023***
	(0.005)	(0.004)	(0.005)	(0.005)	(0.009)
Age-squared/100	0.048***	0.042***	0.047***	0.056***	0.025**
	(0.006)	(0.004)	(0.005)	(0.005)	(0.010)
Female	0.044	0.090***	0.127***	0.226***	0.127***
	(0.038)	(0.020)	(0.022)	(0.024)	(0.046)
Married or in civil partnership	0.038	0.004	−0.010	−0.017	−0.036
	(0.034)	(0.017)	(0.028)	(0.023)	(0.024)

Table A3. (*continued*)

	(1)	(2)	(3)	(4)	(5)
	Q10	**Q25**	**Q50**	**Q75**	**Q90**
Urban area	0.243***	0.201***	0.201***	0.180***	0.062***
	(0.030)	(0.029)	(0.027)	(0.019)	(0.023)
Child in household	−0.159***	−0.184***	−0.147***	−0.122***	−0.023
	(0.034)	(0.022)	(0.029)	(0.030)	(0.027)
Household size	0.028**	0.022***	0.030***	0.018**	0.004
	(0.012)	(0.007)	(0.008)	(0.009)	(0.008)
Religion important	−0.019	0.004	0.064**	0.072**	0.098**
	(0.029)	(0.030)	(0.028)	(0.036)	(0.046)
Year dummies	Yes	Yes	Yes	Yes	Yes
Country dummies	Yes	Yes	Yes	Yes	Yes
Observations	64,728	64,728	64,728	64,728	64,728
Pseudo-R^2	.146	.097	.103	.056	.060

Source: Gallup World Poll.

Notes: All quantile regressions are for 2009–2013 and use bootstrapped standard errors (with 20 replications). Not all countries and variables are available in all years. The countries included are Argentina, Belize, Bolivia, Brazil, Chile, Colombia, Costa Rica, Cuba, Dominican Republic, Ecuador, El Salvador, Guatemala, Guyana, Haiti, Honduras, Jamaica, Mexico, Nicaragua, Panama, Paraguay, Peru, Puerto Rico, Suriname, Trinidad and Tobago, Uruguay, Venezuela. The dependent variable is BPL, which measures respondents' assessments of their current life relative to the best possible life they can imagine on a scale of 0 (worst possible life) to 10 (best possible life). Q10 corresponds to the 10th percent quantile, Q25 is the 25th percent quantile, Q50 is the 50th percent quantile (median), Q75 is the 75th percent quantile, and Q90 is the 90th percent quantile. Household income is log-transformed and in international dollars (ID), which allows comparisons across countries and time. The table reports the pseudo-R^2 for each quantile regression.

*$p < .1.$ **$p < .05.$ ***$p < .01.$

Table A4a. Life satisfaction and future life satisfaction in the United States with race * income cohorts

Variable	(1) Best possible life	(2) Best possible life anticipated in 5 years
Log(median MSA household income)	0.013	0.170***
	(0.0348)	(0.0335)
Poor household	−0.763***	−0.482***
	(0.0122)	(0.0099)
Rich household	0.521***	0.316***
	(0.0075)	(0.0087)
Black	−0.035**	0.705***
	(0.0144)	(0.0163)
Hispanic	0.051*	0.261***
	(0.0288)	(0.0261)
Asian	−0.229***	−0.239***
	(0.0223)	(0.0307)
Other race	−0.135***	0.040
	(0.0190)	(0.0262)
(Rich household)*(black)	−0.203***	−0.283***
	(0.0314)	(0.0281)
(Rich household)*(Hispanic)	−0.060	−0.136**
	(0.0566)	(0.0604)
(Rich household)*(Asian)	−0.135***	−0.098**
	(0.0339)	(0.0441)
(Rich household)*(other race)	−0.067*	−0.147***
	(0.0379)	(0.0493)
(Poor household)*(black)	0.546***	0.401***
	(0.0293)	(0.0241)
(Poor household)*(Hispanic)	0.368***	0.035
	(0.0431)	(0.0554)
(Poor household)*(Asian)	0.368***	0.350***
	(0.0822)	(0.0817)
(Poor household)*(other race)	0.109**	0.066*
	(0.0425)	(0.0397)
South	0.082***	0.048***
	(0.0234)	(0.0144)

Table A4a. (*continued*)

Variable	(1) Best possible life	(2) Best possible life anticipated in 5 years
Midwest	−0.007	0.003
	(0.0224)	(0.0150)
West	0.059**	0.098***
	(0.0236)	(0.0120)
Age	−0.075***	−0.055***
	(0.0012)	(0.0017)
Age-squared	0.001***	0.000***
	(0.0000)	(0.0000)
Male	−0.200***	−0.245***
	(0.0058)	(0.0083)
Married	0.373***	0.145***
	(0.0067)	(0.0073)
Education level	0.124***	0.119***
	(0.0025)	(0.0034)
BMI	−0.021***	−0.016***
	(0.0007)	(0.0007)
Employed	0.215***	0.166***
	(0.0078)	(0.0089)
Religious	0.200***	0.133***
	(0.0073)	(0.0095)
Year 2008 dummy	−0.351***	−0.126***
	(0.0089)	(0.0092)
Year 2009 dummy	−0.067***	−0.046***
	(0.0065)	(0.0087)
Constant	8.000***	7.740***
	(0.3767)	(0.3671)
Observations	468,032	452,913
R^2	.107	.116

Note: Clustered standard errors (at the MSA level) in parentheses.
*$p < .1$. **$p < .05$. ***$p < .01$.

Table A4b. Life satisfaction/future life satisfaction in the United States with race * age cohorts

Variable	(1) Best possible life	(2) Best possible life anticipated in 5 years
Log(median MSA household income)	−0.066*	0.128***
	(0.0342)	(0.0346)
Household income group	0.196***	0.112***
	(0.0028)	(0.0021)
Age > 50	0.021**	−0.062***
	(0.0101)	(0.0115)
Black	0.013	0.707***
	(0.0191)	(0.0185)
Hispanic	0.194***	0.241***
	(0.0283)	(0.0257)
Asian	−0.196***	−0.276***
	(0.0229)	(0.0277)
Other race	−0.067***	0.112***
	(0.0214)	(0.0209)
(Black)*(age > 50)	0.239***	0.199***
	(0.0273)	(0.0216)
(Hispanic)*(age > 50)	−0.047	0.051
	(0.0427)	(0.0469)
(Asian)*(age > 50)	−0.083**	0.178***
	(0.0409)	(0.0411)
(Other race)*(age > 50)	−0.096***	−0.182***
	(0.0346)	(0.0313)
Age	−0.079***	−0.054***
	(0.0013)	(0.0017)
Age-squared	0.001***	0.000***
	(0.0000)	(0.0000)
Male	−0.213***	−0.251***
	(0.0058)	(0.0084)
Married	0.294***	0.105***
	(0.0064)	(0.0074)

Table A4b. (*continued*)

Variable	(1) Best possible life	(2) Best possible life anticipated in 5 years
Education level	0.098***	0.106***
	(0.0025)	(0.0035)
BMI	−0.020***	−0.016***
	(0.0006)	(0.0006)
Employed	0.150***	0.137***
	(0.0076)	(0.0090)
Religious	0.205***	0.133***
	(0.0073)	(0.0095)
South	0.078***	0.048***
	(0.0247)	(0.0141)
Midwest	−0.002	0.007
	(0.0243)	(0.0142)
West	0.058**	0.098***
	(0.0255)	(0.0116)
Year 2008 dummy	−0.354***	−0.128***
	(0.0088)	(0.0091)
Year 2009 dummy	−0.067***	−0.045***
	(0.0064)	(0.0086)
Constant	7.786***	7.472***
	(0.3718)	(0.3780)
Observations	468,032	452,913
R^2	.117	.117

Note: Robust standard errors in parentheses.
*$p < .1$. **$p < .05$. ***$p < .01$.

Table A5. Good stress, bad stress, United States

Dependent variable	(1)	(2)	(3)	(4)	(5)	(6)	(7)	(8)
	Best possible life (life satisfaction) 0–10 scale							
	Ordered logit				OLS			
Age	-0.046***	-0.060***	-0.059***	-0.059***	-0.048***	-0.059***	-0.058***	-0.059***
	(0.000)	(0.001)	(0.001)	(0.001)	(0.000)	(0.001)	(0.001)	(0.001)
Age-squared/100	0.046***	0.060***	0.059***	0.060***	0.045***	0.057***	0.056***	0.056***
	(0.000)	(0.001)	(0.001)	(0.001)	(0.000)	(0.001)	(0.001)	(0.001)
Gender (1 = men, 0 = women)	-0.283***	-0.300***	-0.298***	-0.299***	-0.281***	-0.291***	-0.289***	-0.290***
	(0.003)	(0.003)	(0.003)	(0.003)	(0.003)	(0.003)	(0.003)	(0.003)
Marital status (1 = married/ living with partner, 0 = other)	0.487***	0.354***	0.357***	0.354***	0.503***	0.348***	0.352***	0.348***
	(0.003)	(0.004)	(0.004)	(0.004)	(0.003)	(0.004)	(0.004)	(0.004)
BMI	-0.022***	-0.020***	-0.020***	-0.020***	-0.021***	-0.019***	-0.018***	-0.018***
	(0.000)	(0.000)	(0.000)	(0.000)	(0.000)	(0.000)	(0.000)	(0.000)
Experienced stress yesterday (1 = yes, 0 = no)	-0.892***	-0.864***	-1.958***	-1.260***	-0.965***	-0.908***	-2.099***	-1.327***
	(0.003)	(0.003)	(0.024)	(0.010)	(0.003)	(0.004)	(0.030)	(0.011)
Highest education level (1 = less than high school, 5 = postgrad)	0.164***	0.124***	0.126***	0.089***	0.176***	0.127***	0.130***	0.089***
	(0.001)	(0.001)	(0.001)	(0.001)	(0.001)	(0.001)	(0.001)	(0.001)

Table A5. (*continued*)

Dependent variable	(1)	(2)	(3)	(4)	(5)	(6)	(7)	(8)
				Best possible life (life satisfaction) 0–10 scale				
	Ordered logit				OLS			
Ln (Household income)		0.278***	0.216***	0.277***		0.281***	0.211***	0.279***
		(0.002)	(0.002)	(0.002)		(0.002)	(0.002)	(0.002)
Interaction: Stress and Ln (household income)			0.132***				0.145***	
			(0.003)				(0.004)	
Interaction: Stress and education level				0.095***				0.103***
				(0.002)				(0.002)
Year: 2009	0.232***	0.252***	0.252***	0.252***	0.235***	0.250***	0.250***	0.250***
	(0.004)	(0.005)	(0.005)	(0.005)	(0.005)	(0.005)	(0.005)	(0.005)
Year: 2010	0.352***	0.385***	0.385***	0.385***	0.358***	0.386***	0.386***	0.386***
	(0.004)	(0.006)	(0.006)	(0.006)	(0.005)	(0.006)	(0.006)	(0.006)
Year: 2011	0.316***	0.330***	0.330***	0.330***	0.326***	0.331***	0.331***	0.331***
	(0.004)	(0.005)	(0.005)	(0.005)	(0.005)	(0.005)	(0.005)	(0.005)
Year: 2012	0.308***	0.311***	0.312***	0.312***	0.316***	0.310***	0.311***	0.311***
	(0.004)	(0.005)	(0.005)	(0.005)	(0.005)	(0.005)	(0.005)	(0.005)
Observations	1,659,166	1,246,967	1,246,967	1,246,967	1,659,166	1,246,967	1,246,967	1,246,967
R^2					.111	.139	.141	.141

Note: Using Gallup Healthways Surveys 2008–2012. Household income is at the group midpoint value, in natural logs. Standard errors in parentheses.
***$p < .01$.

Table A6. Good stress, bad stress, Latin America

Variable	(1)	(2)	(3)	(4)	(5)	(6)	(7)	(8)	(9)	(10)
					Best possible life (life satisfaction) 0–10 scale					
			Ordered logit					OLS		
Age (wp1220)	-0.042***	-0.042***	-0.042***	-0.041***	-0.041***	-0.053***	-0.053***	-0.053***	-0.052***	-0.052***
	(0.002)	(0.002)	(0.002)	(0.002)	(0.002)	(0.002)	(0.002)	(0.002)	(0.002)	(0.002)
Age-squared/100	0.040***	0.040***	0.040***	0.040***	0.040***	0.050***	0.050***	0.050***	0.049***	0.049***
	(0.002)	(0.002)	(0.002)	(0.002)	(0.002)	(0.002)	(0.002)	(0.002)	(0.002)	(0.002)
DV: Gender (1 = men, 0 = women)	0.136***	0.137***	0.137***	0.135***	0.135***	0.165***	0.165***	0.165***	0.161***	0.161***
	(0.012)	(0.012)	(0.012)	(0.012)	(0.012)	(0.015)	(0.015)	(0.015)	(0.015)	(0.015)
DV: Married (1 = yes, 0 = no) (wp 1223)	0.093***	0.093***	0.093***	0.086***	0.086***	0.125***	0.125***	0.125***	0.116***	0.116***
	(0.013)	(0.013)	(0.013)	(0.013)	(0.013)	(0.016)	(0.016)	(0.016)	(0.016)	(0.016)
Education secondary school and higher (1 = yes, 0 = no) (wp3117)	0.313***	0.299***	0.313***	0.295***	0.309***	0.390***	0.380***	0.390***	0.373***	0.384***
	(0.014)	(0.016)	(0.014)	(0.016)	(0.014)	(0.017)	(0.020)	(0.017)	(0.020)	(0.017)
Household location (1 = urban/suburban, 0 = other) (wp14)	0.138***	0.139***	0.139***	0.139***	0.139***	0.172***	0.172***	0.172***	0.172***	0.172***
	(0.012)	(0.012)	(0.012)	(0.013)	(0.013)	(0.016)	(0.016)	(0.016)	(0.016)	(0.016)
Household income, int. $ in logs	0.308***	0.308***	0.297***	0.305***	0.294***	0.376***	0.376***	0.366***	0.371***	0.360***
	(0.007)	(0.007)	(0.008)	(0.007)	(0.008)	(0.008)	(0.008)	(0.010)	(0.009)	(0.010)
DV: Health condition (1 = satisfied, 0 = not satisfied) (wp22)	0.628***	0.628***	0.627***	0.599***	0.599***	0.783***	0.783***	0.783***	0.744***	0.744***
	(0.017)	(0.017)	(0.017)	(0.017)	(0.017)	(0.021)	(0.021)	(0.021)	(0.021)	(0.021)

Table A6. (continued)

Variable	(1)	(2)	(3)	(4)	(5)	(6)	(7)	(8)	(9)	(10)
	Best possible life (life satisfaction) 0–10 scale									
	Ordered logit					OLS				
DV: Health problems (1 = yes, 0 = no) (wp23)	−0.139***	−0.139***	−0.138***	−0.133***	−0.133***	−0.182***	−0.182***	−0.182***	−0.173***	−0.173***
	(0.015)	(0.015)	(0.015)	(0.016)	(0.016)	(0.019)	(0.019)	(0.019)	(0.019)	(0.019)
DV: Smile yesterday (1 = yes, 0 = no) (wp63)			0.353***	0.353***	0.353***				0.445***	0.446***
			(0.015)	(0.016)	(0.016)				(0.020)	(0.020)
DV: Experienced stress yesterday (1 = yes, 0 = no) (wp71)	−0.269***	−0.298***	−0.605***	−0.254***	−0.563***	−0.344***	−0.365***	−0.636***	−0.310***	−0.603***
	(0.013)	(0.021)	(0.116)	(0.021)	(0.117)	(0.016)	(0.026)	(0.142)	(0.026)	(0.143)
Interaction: Stress and education (secondary school or higher)		0.045*		0.046*			0.034		0.037	
		(0.026)		(0.026)			(0.032)		(0.032)	
Interaction: Stress and ln(household income int. $)			0.038***		0.038***			0.033**		0.036**
			(0.013)		(0.013)			(0.016)		(0.016)
Constant						4.058***	4.065***	4.148***	3.716***	3.806***
						(0.112)	(0.112)	(0.120)	(0.113)	(0.121)
Observations	94,539	94,539	94,539	93,579	93,579	94,539	94,539	94,539	93,579	93,579
R^2						.177	.177	.177	.182	.182

Note: Regressions are based on Gallup World Poll data, 2005–2013. Year and country dummies are included but not shown, with 2013 as the control year, and Brazil as the control country. Standard errors in parentheses.
*p < .1. **p < .05. ***p < .01.

Table A7a. Well-being levels and MSA-level inequality in the United States

Variable	(1) OLS: Best possible life	(2) Logit: Worry	(3) Logit: Stress	(4) Logit: Social network support
Gini index	−1.129***	3.225***	1.892***	−1.851***
	(0.3225)	(0.3411)	(0.2222)	(0.5563)
Log(median MSA household income)	0.021	0.128***	0.034	−0.001
	(0.0277)	(0.0340)	(0.0278)	(0.0653)
Poor household	−0.763***	0.576***	0.451***	−0.604***
	(0.0121)	(0.0109)	(0.0128)	(0.0194)
Rich household	0.525***	−0.141***	−0.016*	0.212***
	(0.0077)	(0.0112)	(0.0089)	(0.0219)
Black	−0.029**	−0.289***	−0.453***	−0.420***
	(0.0139)	(0.0191)	(0.0194)	(0.0316)
Hispanic	0.060**	0.058**	−0.245***	−0.336***
	(0.0289)	(0.0297)	(0.0263)	(0.0598)
Asian	−0.221***	−0.059*	−0.283***	−0.451***
	(0.0220)	(0.0329)	(0.0301)	(0.0617)
Other race	−0.131***	0.101***	−0.024	−0.531***
	(0.0191)	(0.0194)	(0.0187)	(0.0355)
(Rich household)*(black)	−0.208***	0.052	−0.006	−0.093
	(0.0318)	(0.0374)	(0.0392)	(0.0879)
(Rich household)*(Hispanic)	−0.062	0.008	0.069	0.025
	(0.0567)	(0.0814)	(0.0658)	(0.1593)
(Rich household)*(Asian)	−0.137***	0.121*	0.109**	−0.331***
	(0.0341)	(0.0617)	(0.0537)	(0.0987)
(Rich household)*(other race)	−0.069*	−0.022	−0.030	−0.100
	(0.0383)	(0.0396)	(0.0467)	(0.0915)
(Poor household)*(black)	0.548***	−0.169***	−0.086***	0.061
	(0.0289)	(0.0232)	(0.0227)	(0.0428)
(Poor household)*(Hispanic)	0.369***	−0.101**	−0.144***	−0.051
	(0.0428)	(0.0443)	(0.0410)	(0.0768)
(Poor household)*(Asian)	0.370***	0.010	−0.122	0.360***
	(0.0822)	(0.0751)	(0.0854)	(0.1213)
(Poor household)*(other race)	0.111**	−0.005	0.008	−0.114**
	(0.0427)	(0.0358)	(0.0402)	(0.0580)

Table A7a. (*continued*)

Variable	(1) OLS: Best possible life	(2) Logit: Worry	(3) Logit: Stress	(4) Logit: Social network support
Age	−0.075***	0.073***	0.045***	−0.134***
	(0.0012)	(0.0018)	(0.0015)	(0.0031)
Age-squared	0.001***	−0.001***	−0.001***	0.001***
	(0.0000)	(0.0000)	(0.0000)	(0.0000)
Male	−0.200***	−0.206***	−0.277***	−0.098***
	(0.0058)	(0.0079)	(0.0070)	(0.0117)
Married	0.371***	−0.130***	−0.088***	−0.106***
	(0.0069)	(0.0096)	(0.0076)	(0.0157)
Education level	0.125***	−0.023***	0.028***	0.116***
	(0.0025)	(0.0037)	(0.0024)	(0.0051)
BMI	−0.021***	0.009***	0.012***	−0.015***
	(0.0007)	(0.0006)	(0.0006)	(0.0010)
Employed	0.214***	−0.290***	−0.021**	0.256***
	(0.0079)	(0.0110)	(0.0099)	(0.0157)
Religious	0.198***	−0.004	−0.022***	0.199***
	(0.0074)	(0.0077)	(0.0074)	(0.0160)
South	0.081***	−0.058***	−0.051***	−0.118***
	(0.0185)	(0.0214)	(0.0153)	(0.0290)
Midwest	−0.021	−0.041**	−0.027*	−0.019
	(0.0150)	(0.0204)	(0.0163)	(0.0280)
West	0.039**	0.027	−0.005	−0.149***
	(0.0161)	(0.0184)	(0.0133)	(0.0361)
Year 2008 dummy	−0.351***	−0.033***	−0.045***	0.191***
	(0.0089)	(0.0084)	(0.0071)	(0.0167)
Year 2009 dummy	−0.067***	0.030***	0.000	−0.029*
	(0.0065)	(0.0081)	(0.0078)	(0.0152)
Constant	8.445***	−4.675***	−2.072***	5.882***
	(0.3373)	(0.3899)	(0.3185)	(0.7908)
Observations	468,032	468,939	468,872	240,776
R^2	.107			

Note: Robust standard errors in parentheses.
*$p < .1$. **$p < .05$. ***$p < .01$.

Table A7b. Social support and MSA-level inequality—by age and race

Variable	(1) Logit: Social network support
Gini index	−2.036***
	(0.5642)
Log(median MSA household income)	−0.066
	(0.0698)
Household income group	0.135***
	(0.0034)
Age > 50	−0.183***
	(0.0243)
Black	−0.582***
	(0.0318)
Hispanic	−0.444***
	(0.0518)
Other race	−0.652***
	(0.0388)
(Black)*(age > 50)	0.351***
	(0.0406)
(Hispanic)*(age > 50)	0.222***
	(0.0803)
(Asian)*(age > 50)	0.036
	(0.0720)
(Other race)*(age > 50)	0.138***
	(0.0508)
Age	−0.130***
	(0.0032)
Age-squared	0.001***
	(0.0000)
Male	−0.104***
	(0.0116)
Married	−0.149***
	(0.0168)
Education level	0.103***
	(0.0051)
BMI	−0.014***

Table A7b. (*continued*)

Variable	(1) Logit: Social network support
	(0.0010)
Employed	0.229***
	(0.0159)
Religious	0.201***
	(0.0161)
South	−0.119***
	(0.0300)
Midwest	−0.014
	(0.0287)
West	−0.146***
	(0.0366)
Year 2008 dummy	0.188***
	(0.0168)
Year 2009 dummy	−0.027*
	(0.0153)
Constant	5.695***
	(0.8188)
Observations	240,776

Note: Robust standard errors in parentheses.
*p < .1. ***p < .01.

References

Acemoglu, D., and Autor, D. 2012. "What Does Human Capital Do? A Review of Goldin and Katz's *The Race between Education and Technology*." *Journal of Economic Literature* 50 (2): 426–463.

Adams, J. T. 1931. *The Epic of America*. New York: Simon.

Adler, M., Dolan, P., and Kavetsos, G. 2014. "Understanding Life Choices: Happiness or Something Else." Mimeo, London School of Economics.

Adrianzen, B., and Graham, G. G. 1974. "The High Costs of Being Poor." *Archives of Environmental Health* 28 (6): 312–315.

AEI-Brookings Working Group on Poverty and Opportunity. 2015. *Opportunity, Responsibility, and Security: A Consensus Plan for Reducing Poverty and Restoring the American Dream*. Washington, D.C.: American Enterprise Institute for Public Policy Research and the Brookings Institution.

Akerlof, G. 1997. "Social Distance and Social Decisions." *Econometrica* 65 (5): 1005–1027.

Akerlof, G., and Kranton, R. 2010. *Identity Economics: How Our Identities Shape Our Work, Wages, and Well-Being*. Princeton: Princeton University Press.

Alesina, A., Di Tella, R., and MacCulloch, R. 2004. "Inequality and Happiness: Are Europeans and Americans Different?" *Journal of Public Economics* 88: 2009–2042.

Alvaredo, F., and Londono Veliz, J. 2013. "High Incomes and Personal Taxation in a Developing Economy: Colombia 1993–2010." CEQ Working Paper No. 12, Tulane University.

Anderson, R. 2014. *Human Suffering and Quality of Life—Conceptualizing Stories and Statistics*. New York: Springer.

Ashok, V., Kuziemko, I., and Washington, E. 2015. "Support for Redistribution in an Age of Rising Inequality: New Stylized Facts and Some Tentative Explanations." Brookings Papers on Economic Activity.

Assari, S., and Lankarani, M. 2016. "Depressive Symptoms Are Associated with More Hopelessness among White Than Black Older Adults." *Frontiers in Public Health* 4: 82.

Atkinson, A. 2015. *Inequality: What Can Be Done?* Cambridge, Mass.: Harvard University Press.

Auten, G., Gee, G., and Turner, N. 2013. "Income Inequality, Mobility, and Turnover at the Top in the U.S., 1987–2010." *American Economic Review: Papers and Proceedings* 103 (3): 168–172.

Autor, D., and Dorn, D. 2012. "The Growth of Low-Skill Service Jobs and the Polarization of the U.S. Labor Market." *American Economic Review* 103 (5): 1553–1597.

Banerjee, A., Duflo, E., Goldberg, N., Karlan, D., Osel, R., Parlente, W., Shapiro, J., Thuysbaert, B., and Udry, C. 2015. "A Multi-faceted Program Causes Lasting Progress for the Poor." *Science* 348 (6236): 772–790.

Barofsky, J. 2015. "The Behavioral Determinants of Medicaid Enrollment after the ACA Expansion." Paper presented at the Brookings-USC Conference on Health and Well-Being, Los Angeles, February.

Behavioral Insights Team. 2015. *Update Report: 2013–2015*. London: Behavioral Insights Team.

Bénabou, R., and Ok, E. 2001. "Social Mobility and the Demand for Redistribution: The POUM Hypothesis." *Quarterly Journal of Economics* 116 (2): 447–482.

Bénabou, R., and Tirole, J. 2003. "Intrinsic and Extrinsic Motivation." *Review of Economic Studies* 70: 489–520.

——. 2006. "Belief in a Just World and Redistributive Politics." *Quarterly Journal of Economics* 121 (2): 699–746.

Bendini, M. 2015. "The Effects of Stress on Development Trajectories: Evidence from Peru." PhD dissertation, University of Maryland School of Public Policy, College Park.

Berman, R. 2015. "The Surprising Optimism of African-Americans and Latinos." *Atlantic*, September.

Binder, M. 2014. "Subjective Well-Being Capabilities: Bridging the Gap between the Capability Approach and Subjective Well-Being Research." *Journal of Happiness Studies* 15: 1197–1217.

Binder, M., and Coad, A. 2011. "From Average Joe's Happiness to Miserable Jane and Cheerful John: Using Quantile Regression to Analyze the Full Subjective Well-Being Distribution." *Journal of Economic Behavior and Organization* 79 (3): 275–290.

——. 2015. "Heterogeneity in the Relationship between Unemployment and Subjective Well-Being: A Quantile Approach." *Economica* 82 (328): 865–891. doi:10.1111/ecca .12150.

Birdsall, N., and Graham, C., eds. 1999. *New Markets, New Opportunities? Economic and Social Mobility in a Changing World*. Washington, D.C.: Brookings Institution Press.

Birdsall, N., Graham, C., and Sabot, R. 1998. *Beyond Tradeoffs: Market Reforms and Equitable Growth in Latin America*. Washington, D.C.: Brookings Institution Press.

Birdsall, N., Ross, D., and Sabot, R. 1995. "Inequality and Growth Reconsidered: Lessons from East Asia." *World Bank Economic Review* 9 (3): 477–503.

Blanchflower, D., and Oswald, A. 2008. "Is Well-Being U-Shaped over the Life Cycle." National Bureau of Economic Research Discussion Papers No. 12935.

Blanchflower, D., Oswald, A., and Stewart-Brown, S. 2012. "Is Psychological Well-Being Linked to Consumption of Fruit and Vegetables?" *Social Indicators Research* 31: 103–132.

Blow, C. 2014. "Poverty Is Not a State of Mind." *New York Times*, May 19.

Boehm, J., and Kubzansky, L. 2012. "The Heart's Content: The Association between Positive Psychological Well-Being and Cardiovascular Health." *Psychological Bulletin* 138: 655–691.

Bonanno, G. A. 2005. "Resilience in the Face of Potential Trauma." *Current Directions in Psychological Science* 14: 135–138.

Bowles, S., Gintis, H., and Osborne, M. 2001. "Incentive-Enhancing Preferences: Personality, Behavior and Earning." *American Economic Review* 91: 155–158.

Brunner, E., Ross, S., and Washington, E. 2013. "Does Less Income Mean Less Representation?" *American Economic Journal: Economic Policy* 5 (2): 53–76.

Brunori, P., Ferreira, F., and Peragine, V. 2013. "Inequality of Opportunity, Income Inequality, and Economic Opportunity: Some International Comparisons." World Bank Development Research Group Policy Research Working Paper No. 6304. http://www-wds.world bank.org/servlet/WDSContentServer/WDSP/IB/2013/01/07/000158349_20130107 095623/Rendered/PDF/wps6304.pdf.

Buddelmeyer, H., and Powdthavee, N. 2015. "Can Having Internal Locus of Control Insure Against Negative Shocks? Psychological Evidence from Panel Data." Mimeo, Centre for Economic Performance, London School of Economics.

Burkhauser, R., De Neve, J.-E., and Powdthavee, N. 2015. "Top Incomes and Human Well-Being around the World." Mimeo, London School of Economics.

Burtless, G. 2009. "Demographic Transformation and Economic Inequality." In *The Oxford Handbook of Economic Inequality*, ed. W. Salverda, B. Nolan, and T. Smeeding, 435–454. Oxford: Oxford University Press.

Butler, J. 2014. "Inequality and Relative Ability Beliefs." *Economic Journal* 126 (593): 907–948. doi:10.111/ecoj.12175.

Case, A., and Deaton, A. 2015. "Rising Morbidity and Mortality in Midlife among White Non-Hispanic Americans in the 21st Century." *Proceedings of the National Academy of Sciences* 112 (49): 15078–15083. doi:10.1073/pnsas.1518393112.

Cherlin, A. 2016. "Why Are White Death Rates Rising?" *New York Times*, February 22.

Chetty, R., Hendren, N., and Katz, L. 2015. "The Long-Term Effects of Exposure to Better Neighborhoods: New Evidence from the Moving to Opportunity Experiment." Working paper, Harvard University.

Chetty, R., Hendren, N., Kline, P., and Saez, E. 2014. "Where Is the Land of Opportunity? The Geography of Intergenerational Mobility in the United States." *Quarterly Journal of Economics* 129 (4): 1553–1623.

Chetty, R., Stepner, M., Abraham, S., Lin, S., Scuderi, B., Turner, N., Bergeron, A., and Cutler, D. 2016. "The Association between Income and Life Expectancy in the United States, 2001–2014." *Journal of the American Medical Association* 315 (16): 1750–1766. doi:10.1001/jama/.2016.4226.

Chindarkar, N. 2012. "Essays on Subjective Well-Being: Applications in International Migration, Poverty Alleviation Programs, and Inequality of Opportunity." PhD dissertation, University of Maryland, School of Public Policy.

Chuluun, T., and Graham, C. 2016. "Local Happiness and Firm Behavior: Do Firms in Happy Places Invest More?" *Journal of Economic Behavior and Organization* 125: 41–66.

Chuluun, T., Graham, C., and Myanganbuu, S. 2014. "Happy Neighbors Are Good for You, Wealthy Ones Are Not: Insights from a First Study of Well-Being in Mongolia." Global Economy and Development Working Papers No. 85, Brookings Institution.

Clark, A. 2003. "Inequality Aversion and Income Mobility: A Direct Test." DELTA Working Papers, Paris.

Clark, A., and D'Ambrosio, C. 2015. "Attitudes to Income Inequality: Experimental and Survey Evidence." In *Handbook of Income Distribution*, vol. 2A, ed. A. Atkinson and F. Bourguignon, 1147–1208. Dordrecht: Elsevier.

Clark, A., Fleche, S., and Senik, C. 2016. "Economic Growth Evens Out Happiness: Evidence from Six Surveys." *Review of Income and Wealth* 62 (3): 405–419.

Clark, A., Frijters, P., and Shields, M. 2008. "Relative Income, Happiness, and Utility: An Explanation for the Easterlin Paradox and Other Puzzles." *Journal of Economic Literature* 46 (1): 95–144.

Clark, A., and Oswald, A. 1994. "Unhappiness and unemployment." *Economic Journal* 104 (424): 648–659.

Clark, A., and Senik, C. 2015. "Income Comparisons in Chinese Villages." In *Happiness and Economic Growth: Lessons from Developing Countries*, ed. A. Clark and C. Senik, 239–261. Oxford: Oxford University Press.

Coates, T. 2006. "The Case for Reparations." *Atlantic*, June.

———. 2015. "There Is No Post-racial America." *Atlantic*, July/August.

Cobb-Clark, D. A. 2015. "Locus of Control and the Labour Market." *IZA Journal of Labor Economics* 4 (3): 43–69.

Cojocaru, A. 2014a. "Fairness and Inequality Tolerance: Evidence from the Life in Transition Survey." *Journal of Comparative Economics* 42: 590–608.

———. 2014b. "Prospects of Upward Mobility and Preferences for Redistribution in Transition Economies." *European Journal of Political Economy* 34: 300–314.

———. forthcoming. "Does Relative Deprivation Matter in Developing Countries: Evidence from Six Transition Economies." *Social Indicators Research*.

Congressional Budget Office. 2011. "Trends in the Distribution of Household Income Between 1979 and 2007." Washington, D.C.: Congressional Budget Office. http://www.cbo.gov/sites/default/files/cbofiles/attachments/10-25-HouseholdIncome.pdf.

Corak, M. 2006. "Do Poor Children Become Poor Adults? Lessons from a Cross Country Comparison of Generational Earnings Mobility." *Research on Economic Inequality* 13 (1): 143–188.

Courtemanche, C., Heutel, G., and McAlvanah, P. 2014. "Impatience, Incentives, and Obesity." *Economic Journal* 125: 1–31.

Dadush, U., Derviş, K., Milsom, S. P., and Stancil, B. 2012. *Inequality in America: Facts, Trends, and International Perspectives*. Washington, D.C.: Brookings Institution Press.

Davidson, K., Mostofsky, E., and Whang, W. 2010. "Don't Worry, Be Happy: Positive Affect and a Reduced 10-Year Incident of Coronary Heart Disease." *European Heart Journal* 31: 1065–1070.

Davidson, R., and Schuyler, B. 2015. "Neuroscience of Happiness." In *World Happiness Report 2015*, ed. J. Helliwell, R. Layard, and J. Sachs, 88–105. New York: Earth Institute, Columbia University.

Deaton, A. 2011. "The Financial Crisis and the Well-Being of Americans." *Oxford Economic Papers* 64 (1): 1–26.

Deaton, A., and Stone, A. 2013. "Economic Analysis of Subjective Well-Being: Two Happiness Puzzles." *American Economic Review: Papers and Proceedings 2013* 103 (3): 591–597.

De Neve, J.-E., Diener, E., Tay, L., and Xuereb, C. 2013. "The Objective Benefits of Subjective Well-Being." In *World Happiness Report II*, ed. J. Helliwell, R. Layard, and J. Sachs, 54–74. New York: Earth Institute, Columbia University.

De Neve, J.-E., and Oswald, A. 2012. "Estimating the Effects of Life Satisfaction and Positive Affect on Later Outcomes Using Sibling Data." *Proceedings of the National Academies of Sciences USA* 109 (49): 19953–19958. doi:10.1073/pnas.1211437109.

Diener, E., King, L., and Lyubormirsky, S. 2005. "The Benefits of Frequent Positive Affect: Does Happiness Lead to Success?" *Psychological Bulletin* 131 (6): 803–835.

Drewnowski, A., and Specter, S. E. 2004. "Poverty and Obesity: Energy Density and Energy Cost." *American Journal of Clinical Nutrition* 79 (1): 6–16.

Dynan, K., and Ravina, E. 2007. "Increasing Income Inequality, External Habits, and Self-Reported Happiness." *American Economic Review* 97 (2): 226–231.

Easterlin, R. 1995. "Will Raising the Incomes of All Increase the Happiness of All?" *Journal of Economic Behavior and Organization* 27: 35–47.

Easterlin, R., Morgan, R., Switek, M., and Wang, F. 2012. "China's Life Satisfaction: 1990–2010." *Proceedings of the National Academy of Sciences* 109 (25): 9775–9780.

Edin, K., and Shaefer, L. 2015. *$2.00 a Day: Living on Almost Nothing in America.* New York: Houghton Mifflin Harcourt.

Edsall, T. 2015. "How Do We Get More People to Have Good Lives?" *New York Times*, June 3, A20.

Ehrenfreund, M. 2015. "The Stunning—and Expanding—Gap in Life Expectancy between the Rich and the Poor." *Washington Post*, September 18, Wonkblog.

Fehr, E., and Schmidt, K. M. 1999. "A Theory of Fairness, Competition, and Cooperation." *Quarterly Journal of Economics* 114 (3): 817–868.

Fernando, A., and Londoño Vélez, J. 2013. "High Incomes and Personal Taxation in a Developing Economy: Colombia 1993–2010." CEQ Working Paper No. 12, Tulane University. http://www.commitmentoequity.org/publications_files/Colombia/CEQWPNo12%20 HighTaxationDevEconColombia1993-2010_19March2013.pdf.

Ferreira, F. 2013. "A Post-2015 Development Goal for Inequality?" *Broker*, May 15. http:// www.thebrokeronline.eu/Blogs/Inequality-debate/A-post-2015-development-goal-for -inequality.

Ferrer-i-Carbonell, A. 2005. "Income and Well-Being: An Empirical Analysis of the Comparison Income Effect." *Journal of Public Economics* 89: 997–1019.

Fisher, J., Johnson, D., and Smeeding, T. 2013. "Measuring the Trends in Inequality of Individuals and Families: Income and Consumption." *American Economic Review: Papers and Proceedings* 103 (3): 184–188.

Fleche, S., and Layard, R. 2015. "Do More of Those in Misery Suffer from Poverty, Unemployment, or Mental Illness?" Mimeo, Center for Economic Performance, London School of Economics.

Frank, R. 2011. *The Darwin Economy: Liberty, Competition, and the Common Good.* Princeton: Princeton University Press.

———. 2016. *Success and Luck: Good Fortune and the Myth of Meritocracy.* Princeton: Princeton University Press.

Frey, B., Benesch, C., and Stutzer, A. 2007. "Does Watching TV Make Us Happy?" *Journal of Economic Psychology* 28 (3): 283–313.

Funke, M., Schularick, M., and Trebesch, C. 2015. "Going to Extremes: Politics after Financial Crises, 1870–2014." CESifo Working Papers No. 5553, Bonn.

Galbraith, J. 2012. *Inequality and Instability: A Study of the World Economy Just before the Crisis.* Oxford: Oxford University Press.

Gasperini, L., Cruces, G., and Tornaralli, L. 2016. "Chronicle of a Declaration Foretold: Income Inequality in Latin America in the 2010's." Centro de Estudios Distributivos, Laborales, y Sociales Working Paper No. 198, Universidad Nacional de la Plata, Buenos Aires.

Gilens, M. 1999. *Why Americans Hate Welfare: Race, Media, and the Politics of Antipoverty Policy.* Chicago: University of Chicago Press.

Goff, L., Helliwell, J., and Mayraz, G. 2016. "The Welfare Costs of Well-Being Inequality." National Bureau of Economic Research Working Paper No. 21900.

Gortmaker, D., Must, A., Perrin, J., Sobol, A., and Dietz, W. 1993. "Social and Economic Consequences of Overweight in Adolescence and Young Adulthood." *New England Journal of Medicine* 329: 1008–1012.

Goudie, R., Mukherjee, S., deNeve, J. E., Oswald, A., and Wu, S. 2014. "Happiness as a Driver of Risk-Avoiding Behaviour: Theory and an Empirical Study of Seatbelt Wearing and Automobile Accidents." *Economica* 81 (324): 674–697.

Graham, C. 1994. *Safety Nets, Politics, and the Poor: Transitions to Market Economies*. Washington, D.C.: Brookings Institution Press.

———. 1998. *Private Markets for Public Goods: Raising the Stakes in Economic Reform*. Washington, D.C.: Brookings Institution Press.

———. 2005. "Insights on Development from the Economics of Happiness." *World Bank Research Observer* 20 (2): 201–232.

———. 2008. "Happiness and Health: Lessons—and Questions—for Policy." *Health Affairs* 27 (2): 72–87.

———. 2009. *Happiness around the World: The Paradox of Happy Peasants and Miserable Millionaires*. Oxford: Oxford University Press.

———. 2011a. "Adaptation amidst Prosperity and Adversity: Some Insights from Happiness Surveys from around the World." *World Bank Research Observer* 26 (1): 105–137.

———. 2011b. *The Pursuit of Happiness: An Economy of Well-Being*. Washington, D.C.: Brookings Institution Press.

———. 2014. "Do Trends in U.S. Inequality Matter for Norms of Global Governance? Concepts and Empirics for Debate." Global Economy and Development Working Papers No. 65, Brookings Institution.

———. 2015. "Tackling Opportunity and Well-Being, Santa Monica Style." Social Mobility Memos, Brookings Institution. http://www.brookings.edu/blogs/social-mobility-memos/posts/2015/04/30-opportunity-well-being-santa-monica-graham.

———. 2016. "Unequal Life Chances and Choices: How Subjective Well-Being Metrics Can Inform Benefit-Cost Analysis." *Journal of Benefit-Cost Analysis* 7 (1): 121–146.

Graham, C., Chattopadhyay, S., and Picon, M. 2010a. "Adapting to Adversity: Happiness and the 2009 Economic Crisis in the United States." *Social Research* 77 (2): 715–748.

———. 2010b. "The Easterlin Paradox: Why Both Sides of the Debate May Be Correct." In *International Differences in Well-Being*, ed. E. Diener, J. Helliwell, and D. Kahneman, 247–289. Oxford: Oxford University Press.

Graham, C., Eggers, A., and Sukhtankar, S. 2004. "Does Happiness Pay? An Initial Exploration Based on Panel Data from Russia." *Journal of Economic Behavior and Organization* 55: 319–342.

Graham, C., and Felton, A. 2006. "Does Inequality Matter to Individual Welfare? Some Insights from Happiness Surveys in Latin America." *Journal of Economic Inequality* 4: 104–122.

Graham, C., Higuera, L., and Lora, E. 2011. "Which Health Conditions Cause the Most Unhappiness?" *Health Economics* 20 (12): 1431–1447.

Graham, C., and Lora, E., eds. 2009. *Paradox and Perception: Measuring Quality of Life in Latin America*. Washington, D.C.: Brookings Institution Press.

Graham, C., and Markowitz, J. 2011. "Aspirations and Happiness of Potential Latin American Immigrants." *Journal of Social Research and Policy* 2 (2): 1–17.

Graham, C., and Nikolova, M. 2013. "Does Access to Information Technology Make People Happier? Insights from Surveys of Well-Being from around the World." *Journal of Socioeconomics* 44: 126–139.

———. 2015. "Bentham or Aristotle in the Development Process? An Empirical Investigation of Capabilities and Subjective Well-Being around the World." *World Development* 68: 163–179.

Graham, C., and Pettinato, S. 2002a. "Frustrated Achievers: Winners, Losers, and Subjective Well-Being in New Market Economies." *Journal of Development Studies* 38 (4): 100–140.

———. 2002b. *Happiness and Hardship: Opportunity and Insecurity in New Market Economies.* Washington, D.C.: Brookings Institution Press.

Graham, C., and Pinto, S. 2016. "Unhappiness in America: Desperation in White Towns, Resilience and Diversity in the Cities." Global Economy and Development Memos, Brookings Institution.

Graham, C., Pinto, S., and Ruiz, J. 2015. "Stress, Worry, and Social Support: Inequality in America's Cities." Social Mobility Memos, Brookings Institution. http://www.brookings .edu/blogs/social-mobility-memos/posts/2015/11/05-stress-worry-support-inequality -cities-graham.

Graham, C., and Ruiz-Pozuelo, J. 2016. "Happiness, Stress, and Age: How the U-Curve Varies across People and Places." *Journal of Population Economics.* doi:10.1007/s00148-016 -0611-2.

Graham, C., and Swenson K. 2015. "SNAP Happy? Welfare, Poverty, and Well-being, Revisited." Social Mobility Memos, Brookings Institution. http://www.brookings.edu/blogs /social-mobility-memos/posts/2015/06/04-snap-welfare-poverty-graham.

Graham, C., and Young, H. P. 2003. "Ignorance Fills the Income Gulf." *Boston Globe,* June 23. http://www.brookings.edu/research/opinions/2003/06/23useconomics-graham.

Graham, C., Zhou, S., and Zhang, J. 2015. "Happiness and Health in China: The Progress of Paradox." Global Economy and Development Working Papers No. 78, Brookings Institution.

Gruber, J., and Mullainathan, S. 2005. "Do Cigarette Taxes Make Smokers Happier?" *BE Journal of Economic Analysis and Policy: Advances in Economic Analysis and Policy* 5 (1): 1–43.

Guven, C. 2012. "Reversing the Question: Does Happiness Affect Consumption and Saving Behavior?" *Journal of Economic Psychology* 33 (4): 707–717.

Hall, C., Zhao, J., and Shafir, E. 2014. "Self-Affirmation among the Poor: Cognitive and Behavioral Implications." *Psychological Science* 25 (2): 619–625.

Hart, B., and Risley, T. 1995. *Meaningful Differences in the Everyday Experiences in the Lives of Young American Children.* Baltimore: Paul H. Brookes.

Haushofer, J., and Fehr, E. 2014. "On the Psychology of Poverty." *Science* 344 (6186): 862–867.

Haushofer, J., Reisinger, J., and Shapiro, J. 2015. "Your Gain Is My Pain: Negative Psychological Externalities of Cash Transfers." Mimeo, Princeton University.

Heckman, J. J., Stixrud, J., and Urzua, S. 2006. "The Effects of Cognitive and Non-cognitive Skills on Human Capital and Social Behaviors." *Journal of Labor Economics* 24: 411–482.

Helliwell, J., Layard, R., and Sachs, J. 2013. *World Happiness Report II*. New York: Earth Institute, Columbia University.

Hirschman, A. O., and Rothschild, M. 1973. "Changing Tolerance for Income Inequality in the Course of Economic Development—With a Mathematical Appendix." *Quarterly Journal of Economics* 87 (4): 544–566.

Holzer, H. 2015. "Higher Education and Workforce Policy: Creating More Skilled Workers and Jobs for Them to Fill." Working paper, Economic Studies Program, Brookings Institution.

Hoxby, C., and Avery, C. 2012. "The Missing 'One-Offs': The Hidden Supply of High-Achieving, Low-Income Students." National Bureau of Economic Research working paper.

Ifcher, J., and Zarghamee, H. 2011. "Happiness and Time Preference: The Effects of Positive Affect in a Random-Assignment Experiment." *American Economic Review* 101 (7): 3109–3129.

Ifcher, J., Zarghamee, H., and Graham, C. 2017. "Income Inequality and Well-Being: Evidence from the Gallup Daily Poll." Paper presented at the American Economics Association Annual Meeting, Chicago, January.

Isaacs, J., Sawhill, I. V., and Haskins, R. 2008. *Getting Ahead or Losing Ground: Economic and Social Mobility in America*. Washington, D.C.: Brookings Institution. http://www.brookings.edu/~/media/Research/Files/Reports/2008/2/economic%20mobility%20sawhill/02_economic_mobility_sawhill.pdf.

Isen, A. 2000. "Positive Affect and Decision-Making." In *Handbook of Emotions*, 2nd ed., ed. M. Lewis and J. M. Haviland, 548–573. New York: Guilford.

Isen, A., Shalker, T., Clark, M., and Karp, L. 1978. "Affect, Accessibility of Material in Memory and Behavior: A Cognitive Loop?" *Journal of Personality and Social Psychology* 36: 1–12.

Jackson, J. 2015. "The Role of Well-Being Measures in Minority Aging Research." Presentation to National Institutes of Aging Conference on Well-Being and Aging, Orlando, November 18.

Jones, J. 2015. "Perceptions of Tax Fairness Diverging by Income in U.S." Gallup Poll Social Series, April 14. http://www.gallup.com/poll/182423/perceptions-tax-fairness-diverging-income.aspx.

Kahneman, D., and Deaton, A. 2010. "High Income Improves Evaluation of Life but Not Emotional Well-Being." *Proceedings of the National Academy of Sciences* 107 (38): 16489–16493.

Kahneman, D., and Tversky, A. 1979. "Prospect Theory: An Analysis of Decision under Risk." *Econometrica* 47 (2): 263–291.

Kearney, M., and Levine, P. 2015. "Income Inequality, Social Mobility, and the Decision to Drop Out of High School." Research papers, Department of Economics, University of Maryland.

Keiger, D. 2015a. "The End of the End of the Line." *Johns Hopkins Magazine* 7 (4): 42–51.

———. 2015b. "Kathryn Edin Reveals the Lives of People Who Live on $2 a Day." *Johns Hopkins Magazine*, Winter, 24–36.

Kifle, T. 2013. "Relative Income and Job Satisfaction: Evidence from Australia." *Applied Research in Quality of Life* 8 (2): 125–144.

Kingdon, G., and Knight, J. 2007. "Communities, Comparisons, and Subjective Well-Being in a Divided Society." *Journal of Economic Behavior and Organization* 64 (1): 69–90.

Knight, J., and Gunatilaka, R. 2014. "Subjective Well-Being and Social Evaluation: A Case Study of China." In *Happiness and Economic Growth: Lessons from Developing Countries*, ed. A. Clark and C. Senik, 179–201. Oxford: Oxford University Press.

Koenker, R. 2004. "Quantile Regression for Longitudinal Data." *Journal of Multivariate Analysis* 91: 74–89.

Koenker, R., and Bassett, G., Jr. 1978. "Regression Quantiles." *Econometrica* 46 (1): 33–50.

Kopczuk, W., Saez, E., and Song, J. 2007. "Uncovering the American Dream: Inequality and Mobility in Social Security Earnings Data since 1937." National Bureau of Economic Research Working Paper No. 13345.

Kraus, M., Davidai, S., and Nussbaum, D. 2015. "American Dream? Or Mirage?" *New York Times*, Sunday Review, May 1.

Krueger, A. 2012. "The Rise and Consequences of Inequality in the United States." Lecture at the Center for American Progress, Washington, D.C., January 12. http://www.white house.gov/sites/default/files/krueger_cap_speech_final_remarks.pdf.

Krugman, P. 2015. "Despair, American Style." *New York Times*, November 9, A19.

Kubzansky, L., Gilthorpe, M., and Goodman, E. 2012. "A Prospective Study of Psychological Distress and Weight Status in Adolescents/Young Adults." *Annals of Behavioral Medicine* 43: 219–228.

Kuziemko, I., Norton, M., Saez, E., and Stantcheva, S. 2015. "How Elastic Are Preferences for Redistribution? Evidence from Randomized Survey Experiments." *American Economic Review* 105 (4): 1478–1508.

Lambert, S., Fugiel, P., and Henly, J. 2014. "Precarious Work Schedules among Early-Career Employees." EINet Research Brief, University of Chicago.

Leonhardt, D. 2015. "In One America, Cameras. In the Other, Guns and Diets." *New York Times*, August 19, A3.

Lepore, J. 2015. "Richer and Poorer: Accounting for Inequality." *New York Times Magazine: Annals of Society*, March 16.

Lerner, M. 1982. *The Belief in a Just World: A Fundamental Disillusion*. New York: Plenum Press.

Liu, B., Floud, K., Green, J., Peto, R., and Beral, V. 2015. "Does Happiness Itself Directly Affect Mortality? Prospective U.K. Million Women Study." *Lancet* 387: 874–881. dx:doi .org/10.1016/S0140-6736(15)01087-9.

Long, J., and Ferrie, J. 2013. "Intergenerational Occupational Mobility in Great Britain and the United States since 1850." *American Economic Review* 103 (4): 1109–1137.

López, R. E., Figueroa, B. E., and Gutiérrez, C. P. 2013. "La Parte del Leon: Nuevas Estimaciones de la Participacion de los Super Ricos en el Ingreso de Chile." Mimeo, Departamento de Economia, Universidad de Chile, Santiago, Marzo.

Lopez-Calva, L., and Lustig, N. 2010. *Declining Inequality in Latin America*. Washington, D.C.: Brookings Institution Press.

Ludwig, J., Duncan, G. J., Gennation, L. A., Katz, L. F., Kessler, R., Kling, J. R., Sanbomatsu, L. 2012. "Neighborhood Effects on the Long-Term Well-Being of Low-Income Adults." *Science* 337: 1505–1510.

Lustig, N., Pessino, C., and Scott, J. 2013. "The Impact of Taxes and Social Spending on Inequality and Poverty in Argentina, Bolivia, Brazil, Mexico, Peru and Uruguay: An Overview." CEQ Working Paper No. 13. http://econ.tulane.edu/RePEc/pdf/tul1313.pdf.

Luttmer, E. F. P. 2005. "Neighbors as Negatives: Relative Earnings and Well-Being." *Quarterly Journal of Economics* 120 (3): 963–1002.

Malouf, D. 2011. *The Happy Life: The Search for Contentment in the Modern World*. New York: Random House.

Marmot, M., Stansfeld, S., Patel, C., North, F., Head, J., White, I., Brunner, A., and Davey Smith, G. 1991. "Health Inequalities among British Civil Servants: The Whitehall II Study." *Lancet* 337 (8754): 1387–1393.

Marmot, M., and Wilkinson, R., eds. 2006. *Social Determinants of Health*. 2nd ed. Oxford: Oxford University Press.

Meerman, J. 2009. *Socio-economic Mobility and Low-Status Minorities: Slow Roads to Progress*. London: Routledge.

Milanovic, B. 2005. *Worlds Apart: Measuring International and Global Inequality*. Princeton: Princeton University Press.

———. 2016. *Global Inequality: A New Approach for the Age of Globalization*. Cambridge, Mass.: Harvard University Press.

Mishel, L., Schmitt, J., and Shierholz, H. 2013. "Don't Blame the Robots: Assessing the Job Polarization Explanation of Wage Inequality." Mimeo, Economic Policy Institute and Center for Economic Research.

Mullainathan, S., and Shafir, E. 2013. *Scarcity: The New Science of Having Less and How It Defines Our Lives*. New York: Henry Holt.

National Academy of Sciences. 2015. *The Growing Gap in Life Expectancy by Income: Implications for Federal Programs and Policy Responses*. Washington, D.C.: National Academies Press.

Nickerson, C., Schwarz, N., Diener, E., and Kahneman, D. 2003. "Zeroing In on the Dark Side of the American Dream: A Closer Look at the Negative Consequences of the Goal for Financial Success." *Psychological Science* 14 (6): 531–536.

Niehaus, J. 2014. "Subjective Perceptions of Inequality and Redistributive Preferences: An International Comparison." Working paper, Cologne Institute for Economic Research.

Nishi, A., Shirado, H., Rand, D. G., and Christakis, N. A. 2015. "Inequality and Visibility of Wealth in Experimental Social Networks." *Nature* 526: 426–429. doi:10.1038/nature 15392.

Office of National Statistics. 2015. "Measuring National Well-Being: Personal Well-Being in the UK, 2014 to 2015." *Statistical Bulletin*. http://www.ons.gov.uk/peoplepopulation andcommunity/wellbeing/bulletins/measuringnationalwellbeing/2015-09-23.

Oishi, S., Kesebir, S., and Diener, E. 2011. "Income Inequality and Happiness." *Psychological Science* 22 (9): 1095–1100.

Ortiz, I., and Cubbins, M. 2011. "Global Inequality beyond the Bottom Billion: A Rapid Review of Income Distribution in 141 Countries." Social and Economic Policy Working Paper, UNICEF. http://www.unicef.org/socialpolicy/files/Global_Inequality.pdf.

Oswald, A., Proto, E., and Sgroi, D. 2009. "Happiness and Productivity." IZA Discussion Papers No. 4645, Bonn.

———. 2015. "Happiness and Productivity." *Journal of Labor Economics* 33 (4): 789–822.

Oyserman, D. 2013. "Not Just Any Path: Implications of Identity-Based Motivation for Disparities in School Outcomes." *Economics of Education Review* 33: 179–190.

Parker, S., and Todd, P. forthcoming. "Conditional Cash Transfers: The Case of Progresa/Oportunidades." *Journal of Economic Literature*.

Perez-Truglia, R. 2016. "The Effects of Income Transparency on Well-Being: Evidence from a Natural Experiment." Mimeo, Microsoft, New England Research and Development Lab, Cambridge.

Pew Center for People and the Press. 2012. "How Income Divides Democrats, Republicans, and Independents." http://www.npr.org/sections/money/2012/09/26/161841771/how-income-divides-democrats-republicans-and-independents.

Piketty, T. 2014. *Capital in the Twenty-First Century*. Cambridge, Mass.: Belknap.

Piketty, T., and Saez, E. 2003. "Income Inequality in the United States, 1913–1998." *Quarterly Journal of Economics* 118 (1): 1–41.

Porter, E. 2015. "Education Gap Widens between Rich and Poor." *New York Times*, September 23, B1.

Putnam, R. 2015. *Our Kids: The American Dream in Crisis*. New York: Simon & Schuster.

Ramsey, D. 2015. "The Missing Black Millennials." *New York Times*, December 21, A25.

Rasmussen, H., Scheier, M., and Greenhouse, J. 2009. "Optimism and Physical Health: A Review." *Annals of Behavioral Medicine* 37: 239–256.

Rauch, J. forthcoming. *The Happiness U-Shape*. New York: St. Martin's.

Ravallion, M. 2004. "Competing Concepts of Inequality in the Globalization Debate." In *Brookings Trade Forum 2004: Globalization, Poverty, and Inequality*, ed. S. Collins and C. Graham, 1–24. Washington, D.C.: Brookings Institution Press.

Reardon, S., and Portilla, X. 2015. "Recent Trends in Socioeconomic and Racial School Readiness Gaps at Kindergarten Entry." Center for Education Policy Analysis Working Papers No. 15-02, Stanford University.

Reeves, R. 2007. *John Stuart Mill: A Victorian Firebrand*. London: Atlantic Books.

———. 2014. "Saving Horatio Alger: Equality, Opportunity, and the American Dream." Brookings Essay. http://www.brookings.edu/research/essays/2014/saving-horatio-alger.

Rodrigues, E., and Sawhill, I. 2015. "Senator Marco Rubio's Flawed Proposals for the Earned Income Tax Credit." Social Mobility Memos, Brookings Institution.

Roemer, J. 1993. "A Pragmatic Theory of Responsibility for the Egalitarian Planner." *Philosophy and Public Affairs* 10: 146–166.

Rothwell, J. 2016. "Make Elites Compete: Why the 1% Earn So Much and What to Do about It." Social Mobility Memos, Brookings Institution. http://www.brookings.edu/blogs/social-mobility-memos/posts/2016/03/25-make-elites-compete-why-one-percent-earn-so-much-rothwell.

Ruiz, N., and Wilson, J. 2013. "Better Align H1B Visas to Local Economy Needs." Mimeo, Brookings Institution. http://www.brookings.edu/research/papers/2013/03/13-h1b-visa-revenue-fees-ruiz-wilson.

Ryan, J. 1941. *Social Doctrine in Action: A Personal History*. New York: Harper and Brothers.

Ryff, C. 2015. "Varieties of Well-Being and Their Links to Health." Presentation to National Institutes of Aging Conference on Well-Being and Aging, Orlando, November 18.

Salverda, W., Nolan, B., and Smeeding, T., eds. 2009. *The Oxford Handbook of Income Inequality.* Oxford: Oxford University Press.

Sawhill, I. V., and Morton, J. E. 2007. "Economic Mobility: Is the American Dream Alive and Well?" Washington, D.C.: Brookings Institution. http://www.brookings.edu/research/papers /2007/05/useconomics-morton.

Scheiber, N., and Sussman, D. 2015. "Inequality Troubles Americans across Party Lines, a Poll Finds." *New York Times,* June 4, A1.

Schneiderman, N., Ironson, G., and Siegel, S. D. 2005. "Stress and Health: Psychological, Behavioral, and Biological Determinants." *Annual Review of Clinical Psychology* 1: 607–628.

Sen, A. K. 1984. *Resources, Values, and Development.* Cambridge, Mass.: Harvard University Press.

Senik, C. 2009. "Direct Evidence on Income Comparisons and Their Welfare Effects." *Journal of Economic Behavior and Organization* 72 (1): 408–424.

Shanahan, M., Bauldy, S., Roberts, B., MacMillan, R., and Russo, R. 2014. "Personality and SES: Personality and the Reproduction of Social Class." *Social Forces* 93 (1): 209–240.

Shu, X., and Marini, M. 2008. "Coming of Age in Changing Times: Occupational Aspirations of American Youth in 1966–80." *Research in Social Stratification and Mobility* 26 (1): 29–55.

Smith, G., and Oyserman, D. 2015. "Just Not Worth My Time? Experienced Difficulty and Time Investment." *Social Cognition* 33: 1–18.

Smith, J. 2015. "Measuring Well-Being in National Datasets and Public Health Surveillance." Presentation to National Institutes of Aging Conference on Well-Being and Aging, Orlando, November 18.

Spaulding, S., Lerman, R., Holzer, H., and Eyster, L. 2015. "Expanding Economic Opportunity for Young Men and Boys of Color through Employment and Training." Working Paper, Urban Institute, Washington, D.C.

Steptoe, A., Deaton, A., and Stone, A. 2015. "Subjective Well-Being, Health, and Aging." *Lancet* 385: 640–648.

Stevenson, B., and Wolfers, J. 2008. "Happiness Inequality in the United States." *Journal of Legal Studies* 37 (2): 13–33.

———. 2013. "Subjective and Objective Indicators of Racial Progress." Technical report, National Bureau of Economic Research.

Stiglitz, J. 2012. *The Price of Inequality: How Today's Divided Society Imperils Our Future.* New York: Norton.

Stone, A., and Mackie, C., eds. 2013. *Subjective Well-Being: Measuring Happiness, Suffering, and Other Dimensions of Experience.* Washington, D.C.: National Academy of Sciences.

Stutzer, A., and Lalive, R. 2004. "The Role of Social Work Norms in Job Searching and Subjective Well-Being." *Journal of the European Economic Association* 2 (4): 696–719.

Swenson, K. 2015. "Essays on the Relationship between Income and Life Satisfaction in the United States." PhD dissertation, University of Maryland, School of Public Policy.

Tavernise, S. 2016. "Black Americans, Living Longer, Reduce Disparity in Life Spans." *New York Times,* May 9, A1.

Thayer, Z., and Kuzawa, C. 2015. "Ethnic Discrimination Predicts Poor Self-Rated Health and Cortisol in Pregnancy: Insights from New Zealand." *Social Science and Medicine* 128: 38–42.

Trisi, D. 2016. "Three Essays on the Effects of U.S. Welfare Policies on Poor Mothers." PhD dissertation, University of Maryland School of Public Policy, College Park.

U.S. Census Bureau. 2014. "Current Population Survey." www.census.gov/people/households/currentpopulationsurvey.

Van Praag, B., and Ferrer-i-Carbonell, A. 2009. "Inequality and Happiness." In *The Oxford Handbook of Income Inequality*, ed. W. Salverda, B. Nolan, and T. Smeeding, 85–134. Oxford: Oxford University Press.

Venator, J., and Reeves, R. 2015a. "Building the Soft Skills for Success." Social Mobility Memos, Brookings Institution.

———. 2015b. "The Implications of Inequalities in Contraception and Abortion." Social Mobility Memos, Brookings Institution.

Vo, L. T. 2012. "How Income Divides Democrats, Republicans, and Independents." Blog, National Public Radio. http://www.npr.org/blogs/money/2012/09/26/161841771/how-income-divides-democrats-republicans-and-independents.

Wagstyl, S. 2014. "Europe Pessimistic on Income Inequality as Americans Cling to the Dream." *Financial Times*, August 21.

Wilson, W. J. 2015. "The Other Side of Black Lives Matter." Social Mobility Memos, Brookings Institution.

Winship, S. 2013. "How Much Do Americans Care about Income Inequality?" *Real Clear Markets*, April 30. http://www.realclearmarkets.com/articles/2013/04/30/how_much_do_americans_care_about_income_inequality_100291.html.

Wolfe, G. 2013. "Inequality and Adjustment in Europe." *Bruegel*, April. http://bruegel.org/2013/04/inequality-and-adjustment-in-europe/.

World Bank. 2013. *World Development Indicators*. Washington, D.C.: World Bank.

Index

Page numbers in *italics* refer to figures and tables.